THE FUNERAL

Second Edition

A Chance to Touch
A Chance to Serve
A Chance to Heal

In-Sight Books, Inc.
Oklahoma City

The Funeral second edition
A Chance to Touch, A Chance to Serve, A Chance to Heal
Doug Manning

Second Edition ©2010
First Edition ©2001

In-Sight Books, Inc
PO Box 42467
Oklahoma City, Oklahoma 73123
800.658.9262 or 405.810.9501
www.InSightBooks.com
OrdersAndInfo@InSightBooks.com

Printed and bound in the United States of America

ISBN 1-892785-72-2

In-Sight Books, Inc.
Since 1979 Grief & Elder Care Resources

3/10

Dedicated To

Arnold Dodge
Funeral Service has never had a better
friend, and neither have I

"We" Squared

I love to write in the first person. I like to talk about you, me, us and we instead of the normal they or some professional title. This makes my books seem more personal and warm. That has never been a problem until I started writing this book.

I was a pastor for thirty-seven years, so when I talk about the clergy I am a "we".

I have always been deeply involved in the funeral process. My best friend in high school worked at a funeral home and became a mortician. I spent many nights of my youth hanging out with him among the dead. In my pastorates I was always good friends with the funeral directors. I have helped them embalm, make ambulance runs, and go to the home to remove the body when a death happened. For a brief time, I was part owner of a funeral home. When I talk about funeral directors I am a "we".

Welcome to the world of "We" squared.

– Doug

Table of Contents

Section I The Value of the Funeral

Section II The Challenges

Section I

The Value of the Funeral

The very first step towards success in any occupation is to become interested in it.
– Sir William Osler

Chapter One

The Value of a Funeral

I have watched the movement away from the traditional funeral with a deepening sense of sorrow and foreboding. There is a growing perception that the funeral is barbaric and plastic, and that funeral directors are charlatans preying on families when they are the most vulnerable. The idea seems to be that since a person can be buried in a cardboard box, anything more than that is a waste of money and a rip-off. Articles blasting funeral service appear in major publications on an increasingly regular basis. These articles take the most extreme examples possible and pass them off as the norm. Publications that have always held themselves to a high standard for reporting are now willing to use the same type of writing as the muckraking tabloids in order to blast the funeral profession.

There is also a growing perception that sophisticated people are somehow above the need for a public expression of grief. It is considered "more civilized" to take care of such things in a more private manner. The loved one is quietly "disposed" of with no fuss. Anything else is considered gauche and undignified.

I wish Jackie Kennedy had cried at her husband's funeral. We have the image of her standing on the steps of the capital in stoic silence while John John saluted his father. The whole world gushed about how strong she was, and talked about how much dignity and sophistication she showed in her dealing with this tragic death. That has become our model. Classy people don't cry. Dignity allows for no public showing of grief. To cry is a sign of weakness. To really break down is just not done in cultured circles.

I have not only observed these perceptions as they developed, I have lived with the results. My brother died and disappeared. His body was removed from the emergency room within minutes of his death and transferred to a crematorium where he was cremated. No one saw him after his death. A few days later we gathered in a military chapel on the base where he served and held a twenty minute memorial service. The service had to be done in twenty minutes because an honor guard was to present the military ceremony at the end. When the service was over we moved to the officer's club for a cocktail party.

I had to officiate at my brother's funeral. I did not want to do that, but there was no one else. He had no church affiliation and no clergy person to call. Someone remarked that doing the service must have been one of the hardest things I have ever been called upon to do. I responded that it was not hard at all, but I wish it had been. We gathered together to act like no one had died. The whole service was a process of denial. My mother did not shed a tear at her son's funeral.

The cocktail party was strained and unreal. I expected this to be different than other such gatherings, but it was not. We stood around and made small talk, denying that anything had happened. My brother's death became the elephant in the room no one dare notice.

My brother wanted this kind of service because he was convinced that this would be easier on his family. A leading columnist wrote recently that his friend had chosen this kind of service instead of the "normal three hanky jobs that are so hard on the family." That is the current perception and that is how my brother saw it.

My brother was right. It was easier on the family. Denial is always easier than reality. The funeral itself was not hard at all. Had he chosen a normal funeral there would have been much more crying and more public display. But to determine if this is truly easier on the family we must look beyond the service itself. When a family comes to me for help in their grief journey I begin by asking them to tell me about the funeral. If they had a minimal and very private affair, I know my work will be much longer and more difficult. Most often it means the family entered their grief closed off from friends and in denial. If they start off closed and in denial it is very difficult for them to be comfortable opening up and facing reality in our sessions together.

I still wish I could have had a time of saying good-bye to my brother. I can identify with some of the feelings of the families who have loved ones missing in action. They just disappeared and left an empty place that we find harder to fill because of the lack of closure and good-byes.

My brother's wife died within four years of her husband. Until almost the day of her death she was still calling me in the middle of the night crying about her loss. Her grief was still as fresh as it was the days after the funeral. When the denial could hold no longer and she had to face the loss, she found it much harder to do than most of the people I deal with. That could have been caused by other factors of course, but from the many late night calls we shared I grew more and more convinced that a good part of her problem was based on his disappearing. I have nothing against cremation. I have a lot of things against making bodies disappear.

I have been deeply involved with the grieving process for over thirty years. My interest started when I realized that as a minister I was totally ignorant about the grieving process and that I was doing a very bad job helping people through their grief. A young couple's daughter died suddenly and the mother was hysterical. Her husband and the doctor were trying to get her to calm down. She stepped back and said, "Don't take my grief away from me, I deserve it and I am going to have it." That statement went through me like a knife. I realized that was what I had been doing. That was how I saw my job. My job was to cheer people up. My job was to keep them from crying. If I could get a family through the funeral without tears, I thought I had done a masterful job.

I was forced to face my ignorance and was determined to do something about it. That was in the early seventies so there were very few books available to read. I read all that I could find and the total was less than six. At that time I had never heard of such a thing as a self-help group on any subject, much less one dealing with grief. Without any guidance, I decided to gather a group of people who had recently suffered a death and begin what must be one of the earliest grief groups ever formed. All I knew to do was listen. Listening proved to be all these folks needed and it proved to be the best way for me to become educated about the grieving process. After a few years of this I began to write books on the subject and have spent almost half of my life writing and speaking about grief.

The longer I am involved with grieving people, the longer I study the process and communicate with others who are also involved in studying the process of grief, the more convinced I am that the funeral is a vital tool in the process of grief. When I started this chapter I said I had a deepening sense of fear and sorrow over the loss of the funeral. That fear and sorrow comes from the fact that I think the funeral, done right, is vital to the healing of broken hearts.

My brother's death and the experiences I have had walking with families in grief led me to try to explore what a funeral needs to do to help people in their grief. To me, that is the bottom line. If the funeral helps people find healing then it has value. If it does not do so then it is just an ordeal forced on us by traditions. In my quest I have discovered several needs that can be uniquely met by a well done funeral. These needs are vital to a healthy grieving process.

Chapter Two

The Value of Safety

If you boiled down everything most of the authors of grief books have written, it would boil down to permission to grieve. It is hard to find permission. Someone always seems to be there trying to take our grief away. It is hard to give ourselves permission. Most have no idea how grief should feel, how we should act or how long it should last, so we end up fighting ourselves because we are not "doing better". The best thing to do with grief is grieve, but finding the place and the people where that can happen is most difficult.

At the cocktail party after my brother's funeral, someone said they thought I was doing very well. I told them I was not doing well at all. I said, "If I were doing well with my grief I would be crumpled up in the corner crying my eyes out. That is when we are doing well with our grief, not when we are standing here acting like nobody has died."

That concept of grief seems to run contrary to our very makeup. As soon as someone starts to cry we automatically begin trying to get them to stop. Not only are we convinced that tears are hard on people, we are also very uncomfortable when they are present. Most of us feel compelled to try to say words that will make the hurt go away. We begin explaining new ways to look at the loss. To show how much worse it could have been. To remind the person how much better off the loved one is now. To make up things to say about why God allowed this to happen.

The normal pattern we follow is first to explain: "You know the person is better off now. It's a blessing that your loved one is not suffering." If explanations do not work, we then try to argue: "Now you cannot let yourself think that way. You must get hold of yourself. You need to think of the good times and not dwell on the bad." If that doesn't work, we tend to criticize: "You are not trying to get well. You are just wallowing in your grief. It is time to put the past behind you and get on with your life." We do this with the best of intentions. We want to help and we are uncomfortable. That combination leads us to try to control and guide folks away from grieving in front of us.

People in grief need safety. They need safe places and safe people. People who will not try to "fix" it or tell them how they should, or should not, feel. Places where grief is accepted as normal and even healthy.

I think I was being trained for this work all of my life. When I was fifteen there was a girl in our town named Alberta McBride who I thought was the most beautiful girl in the whole world. She was older than I, so all I could do was worship from afar, but worship I did. After her high school graduation she was on her way to a party and was killed when a train hit her car. That happened in the late '40s. In those days we did not talk about people after they died. To do so was seen as failing to show proper respect. We certainly did not talk about the person to the family involved. Looking back I realize we locked people in a prison of silence and never let them talk or deal with their grief.

The McBrides walked into the grocery store where I worked and I blurted out that I thought Alberta was the most beautiful girl I had ever seen. I realized immediately that I had just committed a horrible social faux pas and did not know whether to apologize or simply run away. Before I could do either, Mrs. McBride hugged me. We did not do much hugging in those days so you can imagine how shocked I was. The McBrides began to stalk me. I bumped into them almost everywhere I went. Finally they asked me to come to their home and I did so on several occasions. Each time they would get out the albums and show me picture after picture of Alberta and talk about what a wonderful daughter she was and how much they missed her.

I did not know what was happening then. Now I realize the only safe person in town was a fifteen-year-old boy who worked in a grocery store. They found one and latched on, even though he was just fifteen. Safe people are of great value to broken hearted people.

And they need safe places. When we think about it, the last haven of safety for grief is the funeral and I fear we are going to sanitize that away. Why did we build little side rooms for the family to sit hidden from the gathered friends? I think we did so because the family tends to break down when they first see the crowd and we are not comfortable with the tears.

I had a funeral director stand beside me as the family approached for final viewing. I asked why he was there and he said, "These people are howlers. They are going to make a scene and probably jump in the casket, but I have some smelling salts in my pocket and the first sign of being out of control I am going to give them a whiff, they are not going to jump in that casket." I said, "You do and I will kick your butt all over the front of this church." He was shocked and asked me why. I said, "That is why they are here. They came here to mourn and they need to do so. Just because you are not comfortable with the way they express their grief does not mean it is out of place or unhealthy. Let them howl long and loud."

We become safe when we get comfortable enough to allow people to grieve without feeling like we should immediately step in and try to stop the tears or express some platitude that will make them calm down. Too often the clergy do so with scriptures or pausing to pray. People in grief are sensitive to our fears. It does not take but a moment for them to realize who is safe and who is not. If they sense our discomfort, they clam up and we lose a great chance to serve.

Helping folks in grief is not rocket science. All we need to do is remember what I call the three H's. They need us to *Hang Around, Hug Them and Hush.* We need to learn how to trust presence, trust touch, and trust silence. That makes us safe.

Chapter Three

The Value of Participation

When my father-in-law died, my wife and her mother were several states away on a trip. I was called very early in the morning and soon found myself in a whirlwind of activity trying to get the two of them home, calling the funeral home, trying to figure out who should be called, and traveling to his home two hundred miles away.

After I arrived, it did not get much better. The phone was ringing constantly asking for information I did not have. People were arriving at the door with food and there was no one there to feed or comfort except me.

The next day when my wife and her mother were safely back, things got a little calmer. We went to the funeral home to make the arrangements. We were greeted by a very nice young man who guided us with dignity and concern. We picked out the casket we thought best fit my father-in-law. We made all the other arrangements that go with planning a funeral. We decided who should officiate, who should sing and what music would be selected. Later that day I took the clothing to the funeral home.

That night I started a commuter service for the family. The funeral home was about thirty-five miles away and I was the one chosen to drive each family member as they arrived. On the day of the funeral I had duties too numerous to number. All of this was tiring. However, none of this was hard to do, nor hard on me.

When my father died my schedule was even busier. He died in Texas where we lived, so we had services there and in Oklahoma where he had lived for so many years. As my father approached his death we began having a series of talks about his funeral. We had to get past the "Just put me in a pine box and throw me in some ditch" stage that all men seem to feel the need to say, even though they don't mean it. I finally told him that the funeral was my gift to him and, if he did not mind, I would decide what kind of gift I would give. He was pleased and relieved. From that day on, we had to go through the funeral step-by-step every time I was with him. He wanted to know who would speak, who would sing, who would be pall bearers, and every other detail imaginable. He had purchased cemetery lots in Oklahoma and wanted to be sure he would be buried there. He wanted to participate in the planning of his own funeral and found great comfort in doing so.

When he died, I had the privilege of helping pick out his casket. We took our time and chose with great care. This was our dad and we wanted things to be right. We chose the casket piece from the florist. We selected the songs with the same care. He loved the old hymns and it was difficult to decide which ones he loved the most. We planned both of the services with great attention and felt the whole process was an act of love. The participation had great meaning for us. It was not just something to "keep us occupied so we would not dwell on his death." It was a vital part of our healing. We were able to express our love in a tangible way and it felt good.

I did not know the meaning of this involvement until my mother-in-law died. She was living in Texas so we could take care of her. We called the same funeral home in Oklahoma that had served her husband. The funeral director asked if we wanted the same casket as the one we used for her husband. We said that would be fine. We were able to take care of the rest of the details there on the phone in a very few moments. She died early in the morning on December 31 which happened to fall on a weekend that year. We knew we could not have the funeral until Monday, but we found out there was a large wedding at the church on that day so the funeral had to be moved to Tuesday. We spent Saturday, Sunday, and Monday in our home in Texas biding our time with no involvement in the funeral except some phone calls.

Tuesday morning we drove to Oklahoma, arriving at the church in time for a lunch served by the church members. We sat in a parlor and greeted many of my mother-in-law's friends. Then we went upstairs for an almost meaningless funeral. That was hard for me to understand because I was very close to my mother-in-law. You never hear mother-in-law jokes from me. She was one of the happiest ladies I ever knew and she loved me as well. She loved to say that behind every successful man stands a surprised mother-in-law. Even though I loved her husband very much, I was much closer to her than I was to him, and yet her funeral was almost meaningless to me. I did not shed a tear. It seemed like we were at a funeral for someone else's loved one. We were not a part of the process. It was a function put on by someone else. We were just spectators at the event. When participation is not there, there seems to be a lack of connection for the family.

We are hearing more and more about the need to "personalize" the funeral. Most of the time that means things like picture boards and other mementos at the funeral. Personalization, as you will hear many times in this book, is more than products. Personalization also means allowing the family to participate in the whole process in whatever degree they desire and are comfortable doing. Take away participation and the picture boards don't mean much.

Participation is a way of showing love. We will discover in a later chapter that people need to establish the significance of their loved one. The participation is a wonderful way to begin this process. Picking out just the right casket brings to mind how much love was there. Carefully planning the service leads to examining what the relationship meant.

Participation helps us face reality. As we involve ourselves in the process, the death becomes real. That may sound harsh and hard on the family, but the reality turns our grieving loose and releases our feelings. It is the first step toward healing.

Participation draws the family into the process. Families will usually build barriers between each other and try to act stronger than they are. I don't want to tell my brother how much I hurt until I know how much he hurts, so I say nothing. The participation will usually break down these barriers and the family will begin grieving in front of one another.

Of course there will be those times when the family will not agree and there may even be arguments over the choices. That is not all bad. Most of the time the choices are not the issue, they are just safe things to argue about and release some tensions. The only time my mother's family ever fought was during the funeral process for my grandmother. They cleared the air and it was ultimately a healthy thing.

It is not only important to say that participation should happen. It is also important to realize there is no other way to offer participation to a family except through the funeral. When there is no funeral, all of the benefits of participation are not available.

The importance of participation has some ramifications to our emphasis on pre-need. I believe we need to stop selling pre-need on the basis that it saves the family from having to make very difficult decisions at the time of a death. The way our advertisements and our approach are worded makes it sound like funerals are hard on families. We wonder where the idea originated that just having the body cremated and holding a very limited memorial service was easier on the family. It originated from **us**. We constantly present the idea that this is a very trying time and we must have all of the plans made ahead of time.

Funerals are not hard on families. If they are then let's stop having them. Funerals are healing events and part of that healing comes from the family participating and making decisions. There are plenty of other reasons to sell pre-need plans, without presenting such a negative picture of the funeral process.

We should also take care not to make so many plans and have them so set in stone that the family either has nothing to do, has no choices to make, or find the plans so set in stone they dare not make any changes, and feel guilty if they cannot fulfill each demand.

Chapter Four

The Value of Roots

When Hitler set out to destroy the Polish Jews, one of the first things he did was dig up their cemeteries. I learned about that from a woman who had many loved ones buried in one of the cemeteries he destroyed. She said she felt like a motherless child with no connection with her roots or her past. It became so important to her that she made a trip to Poland and found one great-great grandfather whose grave had been overlooked and not destroyed. She said it was like finding a long lost parent.

Hitler sent tanks into the Krakow cemetery and blew the markers to pieces. After the war the Jewish people spent untold hours putting the markers together like giant puzzles. The pieces they could not find a place for were put into a wall that runs through the cemetery. I am told that someone is available at all times to tell the story of the wall and the reconstruction. They understood that roots mattered.

It may sound romantic or dramatic to throw the cremated remains off of some mountain or out of an airplane, but I tell families not to throw all of them. Save some to be placed where they can be remembered and honored. Future generations need a place. Future generations need a connection with their roots. An old monk was asked why he cared for the grave markers with such loving care and he answered, "So they will always have their names." No one is dead until they are forgotten. These places mean they will never be forgotten.

I walked with a man named Bob for the final year of his life. His plan was to be cremated and his ashes spread in Las Vegas, Nevada in front of the Horseshoe Casino. When he died the family asked if I could go with them to officiate in some way at the event. I could not go for several months and they agreed to wait. I really think if families will wait six months before scattering remains they will never scatter them. The day after Memorial day Bob's wife, Florence, called me and said, "I need a place. I wish I had a body, but I need a place. Would you go with me to pick out a place?" We found a burial plot and a marker for the ashes. She even bought a granite bench with his name carved on it. We had a full fledged second funeral when we placed Bob's remains in final repose.

I had the honor of touring Arlington Cemetery shortly after the 9/11 terrorist attack. The cemetery is very near the Pentagon and the damage there was still quite evident. The tour was conducted by the superintendent of the cemetery and I was amazed at the care they take to insure that every piece of every body is honored and memorialized there. As we progressed through the grounds the superintendent's voice dropped to almost a whisper as he explained that we were approaching an area where several of the victims killed in the Pentagon had been buried. He pointed out that a family member was present at one of the graves so we should be very quiet. I saw an elderly man kneeling at a grave moving small rocks from place to place. Perhaps he was of the Jewish tradition in which people leave rocks each time they visit. I watched him for as long as they would allow, and, as I walked away, I thought, "Thank God he has a place. Can you imagine what it must be like for all of those families whose loved ones went to work that morning and just disappeared without a trace?" We need places where loved ones are honored and remembered.

When Chief Crazy Horse was asked were his home was located he said "My home is where my people are buried." Wise, very wise, indeed.

Chapter Five

The Value of Symbols and Ceremony

When someone suggests to me that funerals are not important and have very little value to the family, I always answer by saying, "Can you imagine the impact on our nation if President Kennedy had been immediately cremated and his body buried in secrecy? Or can you imagine England not having a state funeral when Princess Diana died?"

In both cases, whole nations found healing in the symbols and ceremonies of a funeral. Thousands passed by the body of the President as he lay in state under the Capital rotunda. It mattered that he lay on the catafalque used for the body of President Lincoln. The symbol of both the rotunda and the catafalque were not lost on any of us.

The family and dignitaries dressed in morning coats while taking the slow walk to the church, and then to the gravesite, is still vivid in our minds. The caisson that carried his body, the riderless horse, the band playing music that stirred our pride and tears at the same time. The lighting of the eternal flame was a fitting symbol that brought a sense of closure to the service. The flame gave an assurance that life will last past this life, and that he would never be forgotten.

The same was true for Princess Diana. London was stacked knee deep in flowers, each petal being a symbol of love and pain. The slow walk by her children so they could feel the outpouring of love from the people lining the way. The carrying of her body into the church. The church itself with more history than even its massive walls could contain. A song we will never forget sung by a friend.

How could either nation face the tragedy and loss without seeing these symbols and experiencing these ceremonies?

I have seen the meaning in the faces of families as airplanes flew by and formed the missing man maneuver. I am always moved to tears and I never was in the military, nor have I been a pilot. I've heard the crackle of the radio doing "Last Call" for a fallen police or fire professional and seen the outpouring of emotion from tough, hardened first responders.

Not all our ceremonies are as grand, nor as dramatic, as these, but each has the same meaning and the same importance. When words fail, ceremony takes over.

I have watched countless Masonic rituals and, since I am not a Mason, I did not find much meaning there, but a glimpse at a widow hearing the ceremonies her husband loved and followed let me know I was in the presence of something meaningful.

Since I am not a Catholic, I do not understand how precious the ceremonies followed every Sunday of a lifetime can become when there is a death in the family. I have watched in awe.

I have seen ceremonies that were so personal in nature that no one in the audience even noticed or understood, but the family found wonderful meaning.

A lovely voice sang *Red Sails In The Sunset* at the funeral of my good friend's wife. No one knew that was the song they danced to the night they wed. But the family knew, and ten years later they still talk about what that song meant.

In our efforts to act like no one has died and make it all go away as quickly as possible, we forfeit these wonderfully meaningful expressions of love. Expressions that have meaning now and offer healing memories in the months to come.

My friend Bob, whose story I told in the last chapter, was a creature of habit, almost to the extreme. His eccentricities of habit were well known among the family and he was often asked to explain himself but he never did. One of his habits was to always have $1.13 in his pocket every day of his life. Three quarters, three dimes, a nickel and three pennies. He had a large basket of coins on his desk and he selected just those coins every day. When we had a second funeral and buried his ashes, I asked the family to place the remains into the ground. The ceremony of doing so held great meaning for them. When the service was over, I began putting the metal plate back in place, but his son took the screw driver away from me. He wanted to do that himself. That is called participation. Before he could start the task, the grandchildren stopped him, lined up, and put $1.13 into the container with his remains—three quarters, three dimes, a nickel and three pennies. As I was leaving I happened to glance back and the grandchildren again lined up, got on their knees and kissed the marker. They were expressing feelings and emotions with ceremony they had no way of expressing with words.

Chapter Six

The Value of Reality

I became a believer in the value of a family viewing the body of a loved one long before I started writing about grief. As a pastor I tried to be with the family the first time they saw their loved one. I expected this to be the hardest part of the funeral and thought that was the time for me to be there to support them. I saw this as a terrible ordeal for a family to endure. Over time it became more and more clear to me that this was not an ordeal. On the contrary, families find great meaning and peace in this experience.

I saw them gaze lovingly as if they were drinking in the picture that was to last for the rest of their lives. They would touch the hair, pat the hands, and talk to one another about how peaceful the person looked.

Many families had been through a long illness and had watched their loved one's body become almost unrecognizable. Now they had a chance to see the person as they were before the illness took such a toll. I hear people say they want to remember the person as they were. That is fine as long as we don't have to see them while they are ill. I stood by my father while he died. I cannot express how grateful I am that what I saw that day was not my last vision of my father.

Embalming is an art whose value cannot be measured. It is my hope that we will never diminish that value. I sense the need for a renewal of our commitment to present loved ones with great skill and care. We not only present a loving last look, we present a valuable part of the healing process.

A widow whose husband died in a car crash said, "It just isn't real until you see it, is it?" It is natural to think that this reality is much harder on a family and they should avoid this shock and pain. The reality hurts, but until there is reality there can be no progress with the grieving process. As in most things in life, the easy way can become the hardest in the long run.

I had a friend whose son was killed in a plane crash that took the lives of an entire football team. All he had left were the ashes the airline sent to him. He told me how difficult it was to believe that his son was gone. He had visions that somehow his son had survived and was lost in the mountains where the plane crashed. He hired airplanes to fly over the area looking for his son. The fact that the plane was totally destroyed and no one could have survived did not mean anything to him. He said he could not get past the disbelief and the need to search until he did something he was not suppose to do. He happened to be a funeral director so he knew he could look through the ashes and find his son's teeth. He had them examined to prove to himself that this was actually his son.

One of the toughest deaths I ever had to help a family face was a member of my church who was murdered in a motel room. His head was virtually destroyed with a pipe wrench. We made the decision that the family should not view his body. If I had known then what I know now I think we would have shown the family what we could and covered the rest. A wife and two children had said good-bye one morning and never saw him again. They had to take the word of others who said that the body they found in the motel room was his. Over the years I watched as they struggled to find reality and closure. I think it was especially hard on the children.

Trauma like this does not just go away. Just because the children learned to act like they were fine and put on a good front does not mean the impact of this kind of event will just go away. We have no way of knowing how many cases of substance abuse, eating disorders, and angry rebellion start with traumas that are not faced and are left to fester until they come out in some destructive manner.

There needs to be some method for reality and the beginning of closure. Closure has become a bad word for those in grief. They respond quite vociferously that there is no such thing.

They are right. There are many experiences of closure and I am not sure the experience is ever finished. If closure is a process, this is the beginning of that process.

My experiences convinced me that viewing the body was important, but I had no idea how important until the son of my former office manager died of suicide.

He was only sixteen when he put a gun to his head and pulled the trigger. I happened to be in town that day and when the call came I followed his mother to the house. I arrived just as she was headed into the room where Justin was. I stopped her, and she protested that she wanted to see him. I suggested that she see him that night. She insisted that she did not want to see him in a casket and I assured her he would be on a bed, so she relented and did not go into the room.

The funeral director performed miracles that day, and that night I went with the mother, father and two sisters to see Justin. I am still grateful that we had that time of saying good-bye. Those who complain about the high cost of funerals should experience something like that night. I have no idea what that funeral cost. I do know that that one night was worth every penny.

About a year later, the mother told me she was going to do something that she was not sure I would agree with. She was going to the police and get the pictures they took of Justin in the room where he died. I began to respond and she said, "I know those pictures are going to hurt. I know they are bad. You did a good job of cleaning up, but I found evidence for weeks after he died. I have spent a year hearing people whisper that he blew his head off. Those pictures cannot possibly be as bad as my imagination has made it. I have to know."

She got the pictures. We looked at them together. I waited a few months and then asked her what seeing those pictures had meant to her. She said, "I can't tell you what a relief the pictures have been. They are so much better than my imagination had made it."

I told that story to a group of mothers who had also lost children to suicide. One jumped up and shouted, "There will be pictures!" I said "Yes, there will be pictures." I thought she was going to start home that night if she had to walk all the way. She could not wait to get the pictures of her son. She wrote me later and said she had gotten the pictures. She was afraid to look at them by herself so she had her counselor look with her. She said the pictures were a source of great comfort. They were so much better than her imagination had made it.

In our efforts to protect people, we leave it to their imaginations. I am convinced that imagination will inevitably make it worse. Every time we protect people from reality, we seem to end up hurting instead of helping.

I cannot help but think of the children. For generations we have tried to protect them from the awful experiences of the funeral. They are shuffled off somewhere else during the funeral. I hear people say the funeral would be too hard on them. They are not allowed to say good-bye to loved grandparents because the experience might traumatize them. In our efforts to protect, we leave it to their imaginations. That which is left to the imagination is an invitation to nightmares and struggle.

The truth is, after years of trying to help people walk through their grief, I know of nothing that helps give reality to the experience as much as the family viewing the body of the loved one. That is a true value.

Chapter Seven

The Value of Significance

I discovered a word that has gradually consumed me from a young woman who had suffered the death of a husband while she was very young. After her remarriage she also lost a child. She was explaining the difference in the grief following the loss of a mate and that following the loss of a child. She said:

> *The grief of losing a mate is a process of turning loose, of saying good-bye. The grief following the death of a child is a process of hanging on, of trying not to say good-bye. You feel like the child did not live long enough to establish his or her significance and so you must establish it for them. That is why grieving parents want someone to call the child's name. We want to be sure the child is remembered.*

The word, "significance" stuck in my mind. The more I thought about that word the larger it became. So large that my daughters tease me by saying that I only know three words and I have written over thirty books about those three words. I hope I don't sound like a broken record and end up saying the same thing over and over, but the idea of significance grows larger and larger in the grieving process.

When things happen to us, the first thing we want and need to do is establish the significance of that event. No matter what the event is. If something wonderful happens we feel like we will explode if we cannot find someone to tell. We may seem to be bragging and bore our friends to distraction, but we must share the good news.

The same is true when bad things happen. A woman got on the airport commuter bus the other day and announced to the whole bus that she hoped the plane was on time because she was on her way to her mother's funeral. No one responded but she felt much better because everyone on board knew what she was going through. That was not a search for sympathy. That was the natural response we all have to the things that cause us pain. We need to tell someone.

If we can establish significance we can move on. If we cannot do so we tend to stop progressing, and the hurt can become an obsession to us.

My grandson was crying one day and complaining that his cousin had hit him. The normal parental reaction would be to say, "Stop being a tattletale and you kids play nice or I will come in there and you will be sorry." Instead of that reaction I knelt down so we could be face to face and said, "I am sorry that happened to you." He said, "Do you want to go play catch?" All he needed was for someone to understand the significance of what happened to him. What works with small children, works with adults as well.

I met two sisters who said their mother was the most negative person they had ever known. She remembered every hurt that had ever happened to her. Negative had become the automatic response to everything that happened. I asked them what was the thing their mother said the most often. They said, "The thing she says the most, and the thing that hurts us the deepest, is that her life stopped the day her little boy died. She still has us and our brother died sixty-one years ago." I said, "I wish you would try something. It may not work but the next time she says that, reach over and touch her and ask her how that made her feel." Most likely when her son died no one let her establish the significance of her son or the loss and, sixty-one years later, she is still trying to get that significance established.

If we cannot establish significance we tend to develop an obsession about the event in question. Twenty years or sixty years later we can still be trying to get someone to understand our loss. A hurt that will not go away or a grudge that is carried for years is not there because someone is too hardheaded to forgive or too weak to recover. They are there because no one allowed the person the right to establish the significance of that event and, over time, this need became an obsession. Collect enough obsessions and the basic element of a personality becomes negative.

The hardest part of grieving is finding a way to establish this significance. Friends and family are not comfortable with people talking about their pain. They are not comfortable with people talking about the person who has died. They want to jump in and move the conversation to happier things. The opposite of significance is trivialization. We trivialize when we try to explain it away. We trivialize when we try to put the best face on it. We trivialize when we try to force someone to move on in their grief.

Trivialization always makes the person in grief angry. No matter what is used in the trivialization process, the results are the same. I have been meeting with a family whose daughter was killed by a drunk driver six days before she was to be married. I meet with the girl's mother, brother and sister, and her fiancé on a somewhat regular basis. The father was also killed by a drunk driver six years earlier. The mother said, "Your book was the only one I would read when my husband died. The scriptures in the others made me angry." I found that to be almost shocking. Her husband was a minister and she and the children are still very active in their faith.

The problem was that the scriptures the other books used were the ones that trivialized her grief at the time when she was trying to establish the depth and breadth of her pain. There are many scriptures that heal, but the ones we tend to use, and the ones we are most comfortable with, are the ones that try to explain the grief away. We can tell someone who is twenty years down the road from a death that, "All things work together for good," but if we do that the next day after a death they will probably want us to leave. When we say "God will not put more on us than we can bear," we are intimating that the death is not an unbearable burden right at the time when they are trying to let the world know just how unbearable the burden is.

The urge to trivialize is almost overwhelming. Somehow we have this tremendous need to explain things so the hurt will go away. In the process we can say some terrible things to people. I am working with a woman whose daughter was murdered. Someone has already tried to force her to see that her daughter was headed down the wrong path and it was probably a blessing that she was taken before things got too bad. When I hear those kinds of things, I shudder.

When we face the death of a loved one there are three levels of significance that almost demand to be filled. First, we need to **establish the significance of our loss.** It may seem strange that *our* loss is first. One would think that when a person dies all the family could think about would be that person, but it isn't. The first thing we think about is WHAT WILL HAPPEN TO ME? Can I stand the pain? Who will take care of me now? Where will I go? How will I live? When it is written down it sounds very selfish, but it is not selfish at all. It is survival. Our first and most basic need is to survive. When crisis comes the first thing we think of is saving ourselves. When a death happens the reaction is the same. First we must survive. And we need to establish the significance of our loss. We need safe places and safe people where we can talk about the impact the death has, or will have, on our lives. That is not whining nor showing weakness, it is the basic need of our lives.

A woman heard me talk about the significance of our own loss and told me how glad she was to hear it. She said that when her grandmother died, the first words out of her grandfather's mouth were "Who will cook for me now?" She said she had thought him to be totally selfish until hearing me speak made her realize he was simply explaining his loss.

The second level of significance is the need to **establish the significance of the person we have lost.** We want to tell the whole world about the value of the one we love. Nothing feels better than a long conversation about the person, especially if the one we are talking with just listens while we share the value and significance of a life.

The truth is we don't know the value ourselves until we talk it out with listening ears. We do not know what we have lost until it is gone. My wife had very serious heart surgery and I was not sure she would make it through. I had loved her for many years before that event, but I discovered value in her that long day that I never knew existed. I still don't know her true value, and will not know it, unless she dies first. After a death it is almost like we have to inventory the loss before we can grieve it. Every day we think of something else they meant to us. Every day we think of something else we want to say to them, or do with them, or questions we want to ask of them, or things we wish we had said or done. It is inventory time and the pain is constant. The inventory always requires a listening ear. As we talk we discover; as we discover we establish the significance of a life.

The third level is the **social significance.** That is one of the major reasons for having a funeral. We gather so our friends can show us how much our loved one meant to others. That is why I love flowers at funerals. I give to charity at other times, but I send flowers to funerals. The only thing I remember about my grandmother's funeral were the flowers that covered the front of the church. Every flower said that other people loved her and she had significance in their lives as well.

Paul Castaldi brought me to Australia to do seminars all over the country. Paul was one of the most gracious people I have ever known, but he was also one of the most fastidious. He would figure out how to get out of every public restroom without touching the door handle, no matter what he had to do to accomplish that. He would not touch a door handle. I teased him a great deal about his fetish while I was with him.

A few years after I was there Paul was killed in a car accident. I wrote his wife at that time and also at the first anniversary of his death. Just before the second anniversary I wrote saying that I thought of Paul every time I visited a public restroom. I always try to figure out how he would get out of the place. I have never walked into one of the new designs in airports that has no doors without stopping to think that Paul would love this. The new towel dispensers that work with the wave of a hand would thrill him beyond end. That seems like a strange thing to write to a woman facing the second anniversary of her husband's death, but the first time I saw his son he hugged me and said, "I can't tell you what that letter meant to my mother." Why did it have meaning? Two years later someone was still remembering her husband. That is called social significance.

Chapter Eight

The Power of Presence

My first SIDS death call came when I was a very young minister. I had not only never heard of Sudden Infant Death Syndrome, I had never been called to help a family who had lost a child. A young mother had found her child dead in the crib. When I arrived I walked into utter chaos. Her mother and several of the women in the neighborhood were physically struggling with the mother to keep her from touching the body of her son who was lying on a couch on the other side of the room. When they saw me they began to say, "Oh Pastor, you need to help us. She should not be touching that body, she must give him up." I had no idea whether she should touch the body or not, but thought perhaps they knew best so, with fear and trembling, I started toward the group.

Just as I started walking someone said, "Mr. Lockstone is here." Mr. Lockstone was the funeral director in our town. A well-loved gentleman who had served the whole town for years. If I could bottle and sell the feeling that swept the room at that moment I would die rich. Suddenly we were no longer alone. He would know what to do. He would take care of us. I cannot express the deep sense of relief I felt at that moment.

The rest of the experience was quite remarkable. Mr. Lockstone walked in and did not say a word. He sort of waved his hand and the women decided to leave the room and let him take care of the situation. He looked at me and I somehow knew I was suppose to stay, at least I hope I was suppose to do so. He still had not said a word. He took the mother by the arm, led her to the couch and sat her down by the body of her son. He picked up the body with great care and laid it in her arms. As he did, he said the only words he said all morning. He said, "Now you hold your baby as long as you want to, and when you are through I will take care of things." That's all he said.

I watched her rock her baby back and forth and love him through her tears. Gradually she slowed her rocking and then turned to Mr. Lockstone and said, "Will you take care of my baby?" He nodded his head and took the child into his arms. I stood in amazement. I had just witnessed the power of presence. He did not say anything at all. He was there and just being there was enough.

We have all experienced this kind of power. When my grandfather was approaching death, my aunts, who were caring for him, asked if I would come. They were very afraid of being there when he died. I was more afraid than they were, but I could not let them know, so I just trembled inside. As evening approached, a guy dressed in overalls and a straw hat walked up to the house. The aunts recognized him and told me he was a "male nurse." In those days, before nursing facilities, there were some men who would live with an elderly man and take care of him until he died. He told us his patient had died that morning and he thought he would come by and check on my grandfather. They were friends and he was concerned. After he checked on my grandfather's condition, my aunts asked him to stay for supper. During the meal he said, "If you don't mind, I think I will just stay the night." That is the only time in my life I ever wanted to kiss a man. He did not make my grandfather live one moment longer. He did not say anything to help me face the death. He was painfully quiet, but he was there. We sat together until the early morning hours when grandfather died. I experienced the power of presence.

I am not at all sure that funeral directors know or understand it but that is what funeral directors bring to grieving families. That is how they feel when we walk in. In a day when we have been criticized so harshly it may be that we have lost sight of our own value. If we really understood how important we are to families we would arm wrestle for the chance to make first calls. We would live for the opportunity to be to families what Mr. Lockstone was to that mother.

There is nothing more important about the funeral than the presence and ministry of the funeral director. I call it a ministry because that is what it is. Funeral directors minister to people. You may never know when you are doing so. You may never know how deeply you have touched. You rarely know how much you are appreciated. But your presence is the most powerful value of the funeral.

My father died in a nursing home. As soon as he died, the nurses told us we could go home and they would take care of everything. Both my brother and I simultaneously said, "We will wait here until the funeral director comes." There is a rite of passage involved in these experiences. We needed to hand our father over to the funeral director in person. Our job wasn't done until that rite of passage was completed.

As a minister I was present when people died on a regular basis. More and more often I was there when a person was in hospice care and the family was allowed to be with the loved one until the end. When death comes, the family is usually told that they can leave and the funeral director will take care of the details. I have never had a case when the family wanted to leave. They want to stay until the funeral director comes. They want to complete the rite of passage. Far too often I must tell the family that the funeral director will not be coming for quite some time and they need to go home. I must do so because I have been informed that a service has been called to pick up the body.

I recognize that sometimes a body cannot be picked up until later. I recognize that being on call at all hours is costly and tiring. But I also recognize that when a death happens the family wants the funeral director to be there. If they have a clergy person, they want him or her there as well. There is no better time to serve. This is when we get to share the power of presence with a family in need.

This had an even deeper meaning for me after we lost a grandson. He was born on Christmas Eve and died on Christmas Day. He only lived thirty-four hours. As death approached the doctors unplugged him from the machines and brought him to a room where my wife and I, along with the parents and the other grandparents were given a chance to bond with the baby as he was dying. We all held Isaac for a brief moment and then my daughter, Kathy, held him until he died.

All three men in the room were clergy persons. Three ministers sat there wondering what to do next. We have been around death all of our lives. We have sat with families in situations just like this one, but none of us knew what to do next. We sat bewildered. Then the funeral director walked in. The same feeling swept the room that was there the day Mr. Lockstone walked in years earlier. Someone is here to help us. We are going to be all right. He knows what to do. We are no longer alone.

He did not say very much. I noticed he did not seem to be in any hurry. It did not matter that it was Christmas Day and we had interrupted his time with his family. He told Kathy to hold Isaac as long as she wanted, and sat quietly by. After a time, Kathy placed her precious little boy into his hands. We had experienced the power of presence.

It is enough that I am of value
to somebody today
– Hugh Prather

The Challenges

In a moving world, readaptation is the price of longevity
– George Santayana

Chapter Nine

The Dilemma

Everything I have said so far is known almost by instinct. We instinctively know the value of seeing the body, facing reality and having a time of saying good-bye. Just looking at how desperately we search for bodies after a disaster reveals how much value we place on this process. Feeling the pain of those families who still wait to hear from a loved one who is missing in action from any war is more than enough to prove the point.

A few days after the Oklahoma City bombing I was called on to write some special words for those families who the rescuers felt would not receive a body. At the time they thought as many as fifty bodies would not be found, and it was readily apparent that this would compound their loss. I wrote the words so they could also be given to those who were not allowed to view the bodies that were found. I knew their lack of viewing would compound the loss.

If bodies do not matter, why do we turn heaven and earth to find every possible part of those lost in an air disaster? I have talked with funeral directors who gave massive numbers of hours in the identification and care of these victims. There is nothing too hard, nor too expensive, when it comes to finding these bodies.

We spent millions of dollars trying to find John Kennedy, Jr., his wife and her sister, then we put them right back where we found them. I have not heard one person question this rather strange action. If the family is not helped by the process then why not just identify the plane, assume that the three bodies were the victims, have a brief service on shore and let it go at that? To even suggest such a thing would have been unthinkable.

If viewing and reality are not important in these times, why do we build monuments on shore when planes crash at sea? I recently visited Peggy's Cove in Nova Scotia. That is the site of a Swiss Air Crash. A large monument stands vigil and there is a constant stream of visitors who come and pay homage. I do not know any of those victims, but it had meaning to me to stand there and look out toward the place were the plane fell.

The fact is, bodies and memorials do matter and we know that they do. This brings me face-to-face with a dilemma I cannot fathom. I cannot understand how these truths can be so self evident, and there be a massive movement away from the traditional funeral at the same time.

Finding answers to that dilemma is, of course, the number one priority to funeral service. It does not take a genius to know that funeral service is facing serious difficulties, and that if solutions are not found we may lose the funeral as we know it.

If over forty percent of the customers in a restaurant decided they were just going to have coffee from now on and not eat the food, we would conclude that the restaurant was in trouble. If forty percent of those customers said they weren't even going to drink the coffee, we might think that place is not long for this world. When forty, fifty or eighty percent of our customers say just cremate the body and leave me alone, what does that mean for the future of our profession?

There is also a social significance involved. A nation that does not honor its dead will ultimately lose its reverence for life. If the dead do not matter, it will not be long until the living do not matter either.

My dilemma then is—since we understand the need, why are more and more people choosing to have less and less in the way of a funeral? Why is it open season for articles blasting the funeral and the funeral directors as too costly and even hinting that the whole process is a rip-off? More intriguing to me is why is no one challenging these articles and defending the practice?

The usual answer to these questions is that funerals are too costly. I asked the audience at every conference of funeral directors why they think people are moving away from the traditional funeral and cost is always listed as the number one reason. I think that is wrong.

The problem is not the cost. The problem is that people do not see the value of the funeral. If they saw value, the cost would not be much of an issue. The average cost of a wedding in the U.S. is approximately $30,000. I cannot fathom that folks are willing to spend that kind of money on a simple event that is staged primarily so pictures can be taken. No one is writing articles about the high cost of marriage. There are no exposés about florists ripping people off at this most vulnerable of times. Why? Because people see value in weddings and they will pay for things they see value in. When they see value in funerals the cost is no longer an issue.

They do not see value in funerals because no one tells them of the value. Too often even the funeral director does not know the value or how to talk about the meaning. I am sorry to say that the clergy are also uninformed and often they can be the leading spokespersons for the anti-funeral camp.

The funeral service profession itself has not done a very good job of telling our story. We have a story to tell, but we stand mute before the world. We have no national voice speaking for us or defending us. We think if we speak up we come across as self-serving, so we say nothing. Every other profession can toot their horns till the cows come home, but we remain silent. People will never know the value of the funeral until we learn how to tell them.

I wrote a couple of small funeral planners. One was for people who are going to have their loved one cremated. The other was for families wanting a burial funeral. I did so because it is apparent that people do not know the options that are available to them. Nor do they know the value of the funeral itself. They do not know that the family can view the body and still use cremation as the final disposition. I found out that if they knew the options, many would chose to view, and since I think that is important, I wrote a book that tells them about these options.

I was in a large funeral home recently and these books were on the table in the arrangement room. The funeral director said,

When I read these books, I became curious about the other books in my library. I have a large library and I read through all of them. This is the only book in this place that tells a family about the importance of viewing a body. The only one.

I was flattered and angry at the same time. There should be hundreds of books telling our story. People are not going to know the value if we don't tell them. We dare not presume and I fear a great deal of our problems stem from many years of just presuming about the people we serve.

Part of this problem stems from the difficulty in telling the value of the funeral without seeming to be self-serving. When we speak of the value we can just hear people saying, "What else would you expect to hear? They are just trying to sell me a funeral." This feeling has left us tongue tied and silent. No one talks about the funeral.

We don't have to talk about the funeral. Anytime we talk about the grief process we say the things that make the funeral matter. We need to train some people to impact our communities with support for the grieving. It is simple and natural to talk about the need to establish significance. The idea of a meaningful funeral is implied.

We are therefore faced with a world that does not understand the value of our service and, as a result, are turning away from the funeral. The question is what can we do to stem the tide, or, better yet, turn the tide back to meaningful and healing funerals for our families? I do not see this as a hopeless task in any sense of the word. I honestly think we can revolutionize and transform our profession. It will take some courage and some creativity. It will never be changed by those who are afraid of change and are bound to business as usual. The future belongs to those who say, "Whatever it takes. Whatever battles I must fight. Whatever chances I must take. My business will learn how to touch families." When we learn how to touch, the world will come to our door to be touched.

This is not simple nor is it rocket science. I think we can revolutionize the funeral by meeting four basic challenges:

- The Role and Ministry of The Funeral Director
- An Honest Appraisal of Our Product
- Meeting The Challenge of Diversity
- Meeting Our Own Fears.

Challenges of the Role of the Funeral Director

The calling of the funeral director is
To be there when someone is in need
To be there no matter the time, or the conditions
To be there with words of comfort and concern
To be there to give quiet guidance through the storm
To be there for the final tribute that honors a life
There is no higher privilege
– Doug Manning

Chapter Ten

Challenges of the Role of the Funeral Director

If I could do only one thing to revolutionize the funeral industry it would be to redefine and expand the role and ministry of the funeral director.

When I was quite young my uncle loaded all of my cousins and me in the car and took us riding around. He did not explain why he was doing such a strange thing. He had never done anything like that before, and seemed to have no purpose this time either. I now understand what was happening. One of my cousins was born with spina bifida and did not live long. She had died that evening and we were hustled out of the house while the funeral director came to the house and embalmed her body in the kitchen. I now know that this was not an uncommon practice at that time.

The baby lay in state in the home and the funeral took place in the living room. That, too, was not all that unusual then, especially for those who could not afford to pay for a more elaborate funeral.

No one in their right mind would suggest that we should return to embalming in the home or having funerals there, but when we did so, at least people understood that we were needed and we were there to touch them. Even those as poor as that family knew that when there was a death the funeral director was needed and would be there for them.

I remember well when funeral homes also furnished the ambulance service for the cities. That practice stopped in the larger cities but it was still prevalent in the smaller towns until the late eighties. Allowing the hospital to take over that task was quite an ordeal for the small Texas town were I lived, and it broke the heart of one of the funeral directors who really wanted to be an EMT far more than he wanted to be a funeral director.

Again, no one in their right mind would want to take over the ambulance service again. That one funeral director is the only one I ever met that was not thrilled at the chance to give that task to someone else.

But when we ran ambulances everyone knew we were important to their lives. No one doubted our value. Everyone knew we were the ones to call when the needs were great. We were there for people and they knew it.

Charles Watson was the funeral director that served my family when my mother-in-law, my father, and my mother died. Charles was a bear of a man and could be like a bull in a china closet at times. His shirt tail was always out and no suit could ever fit him properly, but no one ever wanted to serve families more than he did. In less than an hour after a death Charles would be at the front door with a coffee urn, coffee, paper plates and cups, and the register book pages to record the gifts of food that would be coming. He came back to the home to get the information for the obituary so that would not dominate the arrangement conference. He put a wreath on the front door and took the time to sit and talk with the family. He was not the best at comforting conversations but people knew he cared and so they did not care what he knew.

The publishing of the funeral planners I talked about earlier proved to produce a great shock to me. When we began showing the books to a sample audience the first question they raised was, "When would we present these to the families?" Old naïve me said, "When you go to the home to visit with them." They looked at me like I was from another planet, or at least from the distant past, and informed me that they did not go to the homes except to remove the bodies, and that was normally done by either a service or a funeral director accompanied by an apprentice. Most of the time the removals are done from hospitals or nursing homes with the family not present. Usually the first and only contact between the funeral home and the family is when they come to the funeral home to make arrangements.

We have allowed our vendors to define our roles and our customer's needs. They convinced us that we needed to get families into our display rooms and our funeral homes in order to do the best job in marketing products. So we gave up one more touch and one more time of being there. And one more time of the family understanding and treasuring our value.

It appears that we have gotten so removed from this kind of contact that the idea of doing so scares us. One state funeral association has started a campaign to get the funeral directors back into the homes at first call. They asked one of our staff, Glenda Stansbury to lead seminars on the subject with the sole aim of getting them past their fears. Can you imagine an industry that deals with death and is afraid of families who are in grief? Imagine it. It is very real.

I am convinced that the practice of sending people home from the hospital or nursing home with no contact from the funeral home, except an arrangement appointment usually set up by a nurse, creates gaps that do us great harm. When we leave families hanging in the wind to stew in their questions and fears, they end up angry, and they should be.

The church called me one morning to ask if I would go see a member whose mother had died the night before. The pastor was out of town and this lady had no family in the area and had been alone all night. I called her to see if I could come for a visit and she said she was on her way for her appointment with the funeral home, but asked if we could talk on the phone. She began a machine gun bombardment of questions. The answer to each question was "Your funeral home will take care of that. That is what they do." She had spent the night wondering what she should be doing, who she should be calling, until the worry was almost overwhelming. An all night worry will always lead to panic and frustration. The frustration will ultimately lead to anger and by the time they get to the funeral home you have already lost them. They may never believe you care. You left them when they needed you the most.

At the very least the lady should have had a phone call. If we intend to charge people for what we call services, then we had better learn how to offer service when and where it is needed.

In abandoning first call, we gave up one more of the chances to touch and have not found anything to take its place. We moved from being a profession dedicated to touching people when they hurt to one that took orders, sold products, and managed the minutia.

Our Ace in the Hole

We gave up these touches with home embalming and ambulance runs and did not find a replacement for them, but we still had our ace in the hole. We still embalmed bodies. That was the one thing everyone knew we did and no one else wanted to do. As long as embalming was prevalent, we had value. If a survey asked the public what a funeral director did the first answer would always be they embalm bodies.

Then came cremation and, unfortunately, we did not learn how to show families the possibility or the value in having the body prepared for viewing even though cremation would be the form of final disposition. Suddenly a rising number of people are no longer interested in having their loved ones embalmed or viewed. So now we are fighting, not just the loss of one segment of our business income, but for our very existence. We are no longer necessary and, even worse, far too many people no longer see any need for what we do.

I have heard a lot of discussion about who will be our competition in the future. Some have said it will be from people like Marriott or some other hotel chain. I don't think that is valid at all. Hotels book their meeting rooms too far in advance to allow enough flexibility for funerals and I do not think they want to fill their halls with grieving people.

I think our major competitors will be the local church. Every church has a person or a group that provide the dinners for the congregation. It is a small move for them to take over the rest of the funeral as well. The ushers can seat the people, the church office can print the programs, and suddenly they begin to see very little reason for us to be called.

In the church where some of my family attends, four out of every five funerals do not use a funeral director. They even keep register books on hand, are building a columbarium and will offer urns for sale. This is a very liberal church whose pastor prefers cremation and his congregation assumes that they do not need a funeral home.

They had a funeral for a young boy who had a long struggle with cancer and became a well known hero in the city. The crowd was very large and the church handled it with ease. The woman in charge remarked to Glenda Stansbury that she saw no need for a funeral home at all. Glenda told her that the family wanted to sit with the body of their son for several hours before he was cremated. As a funeral director she knew how that body looked four days after death and how it could have looked if they had been willing to have embalming. The lady said she had never thought of that. Glenda is doing some great work in convincing this group that funerals matter, but she is one voice crying in a wind storm.

I could dismiss this church as just one church, but I attended a funeral in one of the largest Baptist churches in our city. The woman had been a staff member at that church so the place was packed. Probably seven hundred people there and not a funeral director in sight. I knew the family well and asked them why they did not use a funeral home they said, "Well, she was cremated so we did not need one."

The question then becomes—what do we need to do to win back our place and our importance to people when they face a death? Maybe a couple of very true and unedited stories will help make the issue more real.

My friend Hank's wife died after what they thought was very successful by-pass heart surgery. The operation went well but she died as soon as they reached the recovery room. It became my privilege to walk with Hank on his grief journey. One day Hank said he knew I was involved with the funeral profession and so he thought I would know how to answer his question. He said, "What do they do? And why do we need them?" Before I tried to answer his question, I asked him to tell me his story.

He told me about the suddenness of his wife's death and how shocked he and his children were at the news. He said, "As soon as they were through telling us that she had died, the nurse asked me what funeral home I wanted her to call. I had no idea but knew there was one close to our home and gave her that name." He made a very good choice, the funeral home is probably the one I will use when the need arises. A very good family has owned this firm for several years and they have a wonderful reputation. Hank continued:

The nurse came back and told us the funeral home would pick up Sue's body and suggested that we go home and not wait for them to do so. She asked if 10:00 the next morning would be a good time for us to meet with the funeral home and we agreed.

We went home and utter chaos began to overwhelm us. We had no idea what we were suppose to think, feel or do. It all became a whirl in our minds. It felt like there were a thousand things we should be doing, but we had no idea what they were or where to begin. Should we call the family or wait until we knew more about the funeral arrangements? Who picks out the pall bearers? Should we be looking for someone to speak? What about music? The whirl was so intense we could not concentrate long enough to even ask the questions, much less answer them.

Sue died about 1:30 in the afternoon. By that evening my mind was full of all sorts of doubts and questions. I began to wonder if they had picked up her body from the hospital, or did they forget. Finally I could take it no more so I called the funeral home. The person who answered was calm and seemed to be detached. He checked his records and said they had done so and that we were scheduled for the next morning at 10:00. I hung up thinking there was not one word of condolence or care. Just a cut and dried business deal.

By the time we arrived at the funeral home, I was mad. Mad because I had to be there. Mad because Sue had died, Mad that they did not seem to care. We were met

by a very well dressed young man who ushered us into
an office and handed us a price list. He then began
reading the list to us. That made me even more angry
until I realized that he was using the price list to shield
himself from our pain. He was afraid to say anything to
us so he just got down to business. By the time we got to
the place where we were to choose a casket, all I wanted
to do was get out of the place. We bought the first one
my daughter said she liked and left. Except for the times
we went by to see Sue, we saw no more of them until the
funeral. When it was all over I told my children to just
have me cremated when I die and not bother to even
call a funeral home. They made contact a few weeks
later to survey whether or not I was pleased. I told them
everything was fine. I did not want to get into any more
conversations with them so I lied.

Hank became one of the growing crowd of the "Quiet dissatisfied."

If you will remember, I told you about Bob in the first section of this book. One of the things Bob and I did during the year we had together was plan his funeral. Like most dying people, Bob wanted some say in how his funeral would be done. We talked about it so often he finally asked me to write it out so he could be sure the family understood what he wanted. When the plans were more or less finalized he and his wife, Florence, called the funeral home and asked for someone to come to their home to go over the plans. A very nice young man came and together they worked out the plans. He told them what the funeral would cost and they were happy.

A few months later, Florence asked me if I would go to the funeral home with her to finalize the arrangements and pay for the funeral. She asked to see the same young man, but was told he was on a funeral. I understood that he was a pre-need salesman and would always be "on a funeral" when she called. She dealt with a different person at every turn and that seemed to bother her. Families want to bond with one funeral director and be guided through the whole experience. At this visit a young woman walked her through the plans and when she finished the cost had risen by $2,000. I did not say anything but knew I would have to deal with that at some point. From that visit on it seemed like Murphy's Law took over. Everything that could go wrong did so. The hospice nurse called the wrong funeral home when Bob died and two men from a strange firm showed up pulling their cot. I got that handled while the family called the right place and the receptionist could not seem to find their file. Bob's son hung up the phone saying, "They have no idea who we are," I called and got that straightened out and the right people showed up pulling their cot. They seemed to only be interested in getting the body out of the house as quickly as possible. The only thing they said to the family was "When will it be convenient for you to come to the funeral home?"

Even though Bob was to be cremated, I had talked the family into having Bob prepared for viewing and a time set aside for visiting hours. It was snowing that night and the funeral director wanted to get home as quickly as possible but she had some papers that she had forgotten to get signed. She pulled family members out of the receiving line to get the papers signed and left.

I sat through all of these encounters without saying a word, but knowing the day would come when Florence would explode about some of these things and I would have to explain. That day came a few months after Bob died. She said she wanted to talk about the funeral home and I braced myself. The strange thing is she did not mention any of the things I thought would have upset her. I asked about the difference in the cost and she said that was no problem at all. Her words were:

I would have gladly spent $15,000 or much more to honor Bob. That is not what upset me. What upset me was no one did anything for me. Everyone was either trying to sell me something or busy organizing things. No one did anything for my pain.

Those experiences left me wondering how people really felt about what we do for them. I took my own survey. Granted not very scientific, but probably more accurate than the professional ones could ever be. My work with grief places me in contact with a lot of people after the funeral is over. Every family I see tells me the story of their loved one's life and death as well as the details of the funeral. That information is very important to me as I try to help them in their journey. I began asking them to tell me about what kind of things helped them and to list the people who gave the most help. I make this a very positive experience and right in the middle of that as casually as possible I simply say, "And what did the funeral director do that really helped you with your grief?" I have gotten the same answer every time. Without fail they have looked rather funny and almost startled at the question and then responded with, "Nothing."

The first time someone said that I almost jumped on them. I wanted to say that they just did not understand the funeral director does many things that make the experience happen, but I did not say a word. If that is their perception then that is the reality we must face. Folks don't know what we do and don't feel like we are much help to them as far as their dealing with their pain and grief is concerned. Either we are not touching them or they don't recognize a touch when it happens.

This sounds rather negative but I am not negative at all. I think we can discover ways to touch that will re-install us as valuable to families in their time of need.

Finding a New Ace in the Hole

The bottom line to all of this is grief. When we are called to serve a family, we are called because they need more than body removal. They need a touch that lets them know we care and are with them in their pain. Every family we serve is in grief. Some more than others, of course, but all of them walk into our facility with heavy and broken hearts waiting for someone to reach out and touch them. When they are in pain, nothing else matters except that pain. When the pain is ignored, or avoided, they feel rejected and that we do not care.

In some of the seminars I do, I ask someone from the audience to help me by acting out a scene for me. I say that I am the owner of a grocery store. The individual comes in to tell me that he/she has closed the car door on their fingers and hurt them bad enough that they may even be broken. Each one will hold their fingers and rather dramatically tell me their problem. My response is, "Would you like to buy some watermelons?" They start over telling me about their accident and I continue with, "We have some red meat ones, and some yellow meat ones and even have some that do not have seeds. Would you like to buy some watermelons?" I wish I had pictures of the looks that come on their faces when I first ask them about watermelons and the anger they show as I continue talking about it, no matter how hard they try to show me their hurt fingers. One young woman had the best response of all. She had her hand up by her face and was really getting into the act. When I sprung the watermelons on her she stopped, stunned in her tracks, and very slowly her middle finger came up and she flipped me off right there. Funny stuff, but that is exactly how Hank felt when he was handed a price list after an all night vigil, or Florence after eight different encounters with the funeral home over several months saying, "They ignored my pain and tried to sell me something."

When I first started talking to funeral directors about grief their response was, "We are not grief counselors." And that is right. We are not grief counselors and should not be unless we wish to go through training and start an aftercare counseling program. Families are not ready for counseling while they are in our care. We do not need to be grief counselors but we better learn how to notice, respond and give comfort to them in a way that shows our care and concern in a way that is appropriate to where they are at that stage of the grieving experience.

Learning how to respond and touch people when, and where, they hurt can become our new ace in the hole. When we become known for our ability to comfort and bring peace we will once again be needed and used by families. They will know and understand the worth of that kind of care.

And this area is wide open to us. No one else that really knows what to say or do is available to most families. We assume the clergy provides this care, but most of them are untrained in the area of grief. Very few seminaries offer courses about grief. Most are trained to read scriptures and pray, which are valuable, of course, but do not meet the need for someone to listen and be a sense of presence. We can become the ones who help the most.

That should not scare us nor make us have visions of vast amounts of time being uncomfortable while someone cries out of control. It is amazing how much just being present for people can accomplish. Bob died on a Monday morning and that was my normal day to visit with him, so I was on my way there when he died. I am amazed at how many times Florence has said she could not have made it through that morning without me. I have given that a lot of thought and closely examined what I did that was so amazingly helpful. My conclusion is, nothing. I really did not do anything except sit at the kitchen table drinking a cup of coffee for a little while. I was just there. I did answer a few questions by telling them they did not need to worry, the funeral home would take care of what they were wondering about. I just sat there for maybe thirty minutes and became a hero.

Buckets

Dealing with grief is really not rocket science. In my seminars, I use a couple of buckets to illustrate the process. I get someone from the audience to come forward and hold one of the buckets. I tell them to suppose they had just lost a loved one and the bucket represented their feelings. I ask them to list the feelings they think would be in the bucket. I also ask the audience to chime in with ideas as well. The responses are overwhelming: Sadness, fear, loneliness, anxiety, the list is endless. Then I ask them what thoughts would be in the bucket. Then what frustrations. I then say that the bucket is full and overflowing. I hold up the second bucket and announce that it represents my in-put. I explain that my bucket is full of platitudes, cheer up statements, explanations, and scriptures, and that I want to stand off and pour my stuff into their bucket. The problem is, there is no room in the other bucket. It is so full the person holding it cannot begin to even hear what I am saying. They are already overwhelmed and their emotions are so overloaded that nothing I say will register. The issue is that I am afraid of their bucket. I don't dare get too close, or open up any real conversations, for fear that I will not know what to say or that the person might get out of control and cry, or the whole thing might become far more intimate than I know how to handle. So I just stand back and pour.

I was doing a conference for Compassionate Friends and was asked to speak on guilt and anger in grief. I asked the audience what they felt guilty about and will never forget one of the responses. A woman said, "All the way to the hospital my son begged me to turn back. He did not want the transplant, he was afraid, I did not turn back and he died." I asked her how many times someone had told her that without the transplant he would have died anyway. She said, "Many". I asked if that had helped and she said, "No". I went through a list of things people have said to her: "You were acting out of love; It has been four years; God won't put more on you than you can bear..." The list could go on and on. Each time I asked if the statements had helped and each time she said "No". Matter of fact, most of them made her mad. Then I asked, "What if I came over there, hugged you and said 'that must really hurt.' Would that help?" She said that would help.

Why would that help? I am getting in her bucket with her. I am legitimizing her pain. I am letting her know that I am comfortable with her tears.

I learned a valuable lesson that day. I learned that healing always begins in the other person's bucket. It never begins in my bucket. There is nothing in my bucket that will relieve the pain or make the grief go away. I don't have to worry about what to say or how to say it. All I have to do is acknowledge the pain and learn how to be comfortable while doing so.

Isn't it strange that, "That must really hurt" is the most comforting thing we can say to someone in pain? That is so foreign to the way we were raised or trained, and it may seem threatening since it opens up the chance for someone to respond further. It should not be threatening. If they respond all we have to do is listen.

At one of our Funeral Celebrant Trainings a young funeral director asked, "What do I say to people the first time I see them after a death?" He must have slept through all the times I had said it during our training, so once again I said, "In your own words you say something like, 'That must really hurt.'" The next day he told me that those words really work. Then he told me he had gone to the bar in the hotel and thought the female singer was beautiful so he asked to buy her a drink. He said the conversation was bland and dull until she said she had just broken up with her boyfriend. He said he had used the magic words "that must really hurt," and things had warmed up and they were going to see each other again. I told him I really did not intend to give him a pickup line to use in bars, but power to him. He sent an e-mail sometime later that simply said, "It's still working."

Knowing Your Customer

Admitting that we know little about grief is like a car dealer who knows how to sell cars but confesses that he has no clue about motors, or brakes, or horsepower, and has no interest in how financing a car works. When we talk about grief we are really talking about knowing our customers. We cannot know too much about our customers. The marketing director of our company, Glenda Stansbury, went to mortuary school and became a licensed funeral director/embalmer with no intention of ever serving as a funeral director. She loves it enough to do so, and currently teaches one course at the university where she received her degree, but that was not her purpose for getting the degree. She did so because we know we cannot know too much about our customers. Funeral directors are our customers and we need to know everything we possibly can know, from what they studied in school, to what their every day life is like.

For the funeral industry to remain ignorant of what people are experiencing at the very moment they are trying to serve them is inexcusable. There are courses of study and materials available and readily accessible to anyone who wishes to learn. Within the profession there are such courses as Life Appreciation, or Alan Wolfelt is teaching on the subject. We offer a course of study called *The Power Of Presence* and the list could go on. There are also all kinds of resources outside of the funeral profession. We could learn so much more if we would open ourselves to the outside world. That is true in every aspect of our business, but especially true when it comes to understanding how to relate to people in grief.

I think the smartest thing any funeral director could do would be to stop and take a blunt, honest look at what happens from the first notice that a death has occurred through each step of the process. It is important to discover when, or if, there is a time when someone actually gets into the buckets of the families we serve. When and where does that happen? If it does not happen, then what do we need to do to make it happen? We cannot continue selling watermelons to people in pain. Making sure we know how to respond, and that we are responding, is job one and should dominate everything we do.

I spoke for a corporate group at one of their annual training meetings. I was to speak in the afternoon so I had the chance to hear the speaker in the morning. He was an executive with the company and did an excellent job motivating his employees. His main emphasis that day was a plea for them to call on each family the third week after the funeral to set up a pre-need meeting while it was still fresh on their minds. He was insistent about doing so the third week.

During lunch I asked the group of executives how they arrived at making the call during the third week. Their answer was that they had been trained in sales and that the third week was the best time to follow up a sale.

I asked them how much consideration was given to where the family would be in their grieving process during the third week. They were stunned by the question and finally said that no thought had been given to that aspect and asked me why I asked the question. I said:

> *Because you could not have chosen a worse time to try to sell a grieving family any product. When grief comes there is a period when everything is a whirl and the loss is not yet real. Usually that period lasts about three weeks and then reality hits. The family will probably be in more pain during that time than they were the day of the funeral. You have chosen the time when they are hurting the most to sell them a product?*

Watermelons redux.

My point was not that the week they chose was right or wrong. My point was that they did not consider the family's pain or need when they made the choice. I think where the family is should dominate every choice we make and every task we do. We need to look at every step of our service in light of where is the family and what do they need?

In the first section of this book we dealt with the establishing of significance. I said that when a death occurs significance has three levels. First they need to establish the significance of their loss. Second they need to establish the significance of the person they have lost, and the last was to establish the social significance. The first two are the ones we need to deal with. When we are called to serve, the family needs someone to hear about what they have lost and how valuable the person was to them. With that in mind, we need to walk through each step and ask ourselves what are we doing to meet those two needs? What works and what does not work? When and how do we get in their buckets?

Do We Touch at First Call?

The death has just happened and the effort to understand and explain the significance of what has happened, and the value of the person who has died begins to overwhelm. How does it feel when a funeral director shows up pulling a cot saying nothing more than, "Where is the body?"

As I explained, when Bob died, the hospice nurse called the wrong funeral home. Suddenly there were two funeral directors standing on the front porch pulling a cot. I happened to notice the mistake and stopped them at the door. It was awkward, but not a disaster. Then the right funeral home arrived. They, too, came in pulling their cot and immediately went about the task of collecting the body. One pulled me aside to ask my opinion of whether to take the body out the front door or the back. The garage was in the back so the driveway went back there and he did not know which would be best. That big decision made, he went on about his work. As they came through the kitchen where the family had gathered the funeral director stopped to ask when it would be convenient for them to come to the funeral home to make arrangements. That was it. Not one word of condolence or response. No chance for questions. No instructions or guidance. The body snatchers had done their work and were gone.

Ten minutes, some training, and a little courage could have turned that into a magical moment. All it would have taken was for the funeral director to walk in without the cot, let his assistant worry with parking the car, take the widow's hand and simply let her know that he recognized she was in pain. Remember, "That must really hurt" are the most healing words we can say and they can be said in many ways, but it needs to be said. From there a brief time sitting around the kitchen table listening to their story and answering any questions does miraculous things. Remember, all I did that day was sit at the kitchen table and Florence has told the world she could not have made it through that day without me. She needs to be saying that about the funeral director.

Do We Fill the Gaps?

I have watched the process from going into the homes to give comfort, to forcing families to come to the funeral home where we feel more comfortable. I have seen the emphasis change from trying to be the most help to a family during this chaotic time, to being marketers of caskets, and peripheral services, and our major job becoming taking care of the minutia.

Our retreat away from the home has left a huge gap in the care needed and the care provided. The norm now is for the family to be sent home from the hospital or nursing facility with no personal contact from the funeral home and only an appointment for the next day. Even if the death happens in the home, the usual approach is for a couple of people from the funeral home stopping by to pick up the body and doing little more than setting up the appointment for the family to come to the funeral home to make arrangements. That leaves a gap of several hours when the family is left alone to question and feel lost while waiting for the appointed hour of their deliverance.

I am not exaggerating when I say the most difficult period the family will face is that gap. I do not exaggerate when I say the family needs the presence of the funeral director more at that time than any other time in the whole experience. I do not exaggerate when I say, that time is the one golden opportunity for the funeral director to once again be needed and his or her work be valued.

Anger begins with disappointment. Rarely does anyone get angry without first being disappointed. In the stories I have shared about Hank, Florence, and the woman from our church, each one was left hanging. Each one felt disappointed, and each one of them arrived at the funeral home already feeling some anger.

No one should ever have to walk into an arrangement room cold. Someone from the funeral home should have made personal contact with that family. When I say that in conferences, I see the audience roll their eyes and the response is always that they are far too busy to give this kind of service. I have three responses to that excuse:

1. What are you too busy doing that is more important than touching families?
2. I have probably been in more funeral homes than anyone I know. I have always made it a point to tour every one possible. I have never walked in one yet that there were not several employees milling around with nothing to do except wait for the next call or the next appointment.
3. Any funeral home that is too busy to meet the needs of the families it serves will one day have plenty of time to do nothing.

We are facing that kind of crisis. Either we learn how to be necessary and valuable to families, or we will stand on the side lines while funerals are done without us.

Are We a Safe Place?

A vendor asked me to look at their display of a selection room. They had spent a great deal of time and money on a new design and were kind enough to show it to me. They went to great lengths to tell me about the reactions they had received from the test marketing process. They brought in a cross section of people to see how they responded and had gotten good results. I really didn't want to rain on their parade but I asked them how many of the people in the test group had been up all night crying over the death of a loved one? Of course they had to say none. I was not trying to be mean, but I said, "Then the test didn't tell you very much. Go study the early moments of grief and then plan your display."

I think we should spend as much time and effort planning our arrangement rooms as we do our display rooms. Is it a warm place? Like a den at home more than a conference room at the office? Does it say, "We are here to get a job done," or "Let's visit together about your loss" ?

Is the room too busy? People in grief have a hard time concentrating and are easily overwhelmed. When a wave of grief hits, the body secretes cortisol which makes the mind whirl like a gerbil in a cage and creates a temporary case of attention deficit disorder. I cannot count the number of lending libraries I have seen in funeral homes. I always ask if very many people take advantage of that service. The inevitable answer is "no" followed by my being asked "why." The reason is that most libraries are a book case full of books and the grieving person cannot concentrate long enough to read the titles. We should have one book that applies to their situation available in the arrangement room, not a bookcase full.

A friend showed me his arrangement room which was his pride and joy. He had moved it from a wonderfully warm and quiet room to a much larger area so he could display products ranging from register books to gift items, with one part of the room featuring the casket display. I did not want to dim his enthusiasm but I could not imagine what it must be like for a grieving family to walk into that area. It overwhelmed me, and I was not there to arrange a funeral for someone I loved. I uttered no negative comment but began walking around the room picking up pieces from the various areas and asking if the families purchased very many of them. His answer was that they did not do so, but he kept them their for their ambiance. To a grieving family warm, personal and uncluttered feels safe. Busy, brash and "buy me now" overwhelms and feels like pressure.

The First Words

I cannot begin to count the number of times funeral directors have admitted they have no idea what to say to a grieving family. I cannot count how many times I have been asked what should be said. Earlier in this section I told about getting into their buckets and suggested our first words should be, "That must really hurt." Though that thought can be worded many ways, our first response needs to be an acknowledgement of their pain. My answer seems to scare funeral directors more than it helps them. Let's face it, just because we deal with grief every day, does not mean we are comfortable being around it. Just because families cry at our place does not mean the tears do not frighten us.

That creates a major problem in our quest to discover new ways to touch families. The first need the family has is to establish the significance of their loss. They do that by sharing the experience with someone with an empathetic ear. Since such a large number of funeral directors find that to be frightening or so uncomfortable for them, we are almost at a stalemate. This became so evident to us and was so important to us that we developed a series of short DVDs for the funeral director to watch with the family. The DVDs are specific to the types of losses: baby, child, long-term illness, tragic circumstances, suicide, or any loss. Our hope was that watching the videos would train the funeral director in what to say and gradually build confidence and comfort in dealing with even the most difficult situations. We also hoped that funeral directors who just cannot get comfortable dealing with these kinds of issues would simply play the tape for the family before proceeding to the business of arrangements. Those DVDs may or may not prove to be an answer, but somewhere, somehow we must find an answer. We cannot stand many more cases like Hank and his funeral director using the price list as a shield to keep from dealing with the grief.

Care That Continues

I heard a marketing guru say that an aftercare program was a waste of time and money. Yeah, who would want a family to go away thinking the funeral home was there to help them and not to just sell them something? Who on earth would want a family telling others they could not have made it through their grief without the help of those wonderful people at the funeral home? My gosh, if we are not careful someone might get the horrible idea that we really are a valuable source for families during their grieving experience. According to that speaker we would be much better off bombarding families with surveys and pre-need salespersons than offering something that gives healing to hurting families after we have helped them through the funeral experience.

I don't know about anyone else, but requests for me to fill out some survey because I did business with some motel, store, or airline is a major irritant to me. If they would spend half as much time being sure they gave great service as they do trying to check up on the result of untrained and non-caring employees, they might not need a survey. A funeral home that gets more than ten percent return on survey request is rare indeed. Even if they get twenty percent that still leaves eighty percent of the families they served throwing the thing in the trash. What percent throw their aftercare materials away?

Again, if I could do only one thing to change and revitalize the funeral industry it would be to redefine and elevate the role and ministry of the funeral director. That is the only way we can change our focus from a marketing model to a service model. Ultimately, service will be all we have to market.

Challenge
of our
Product

*The way to develop self-confidence
is to do the thing you fear
and get a record of successful
experiences behind you.
– William Jennings Bryan*

Chapter Eleven

The Challenge of Our Product

Let's face it. We sell a product people do not want to buy; they buy it because they have to. Because we sell a product people need to buy, even if they don't want to, we have not bothered to change or improve it for the past fifty years. Suddenly people are realizing they do not have to buy our product, and we are left wondering what happened.

That is tough because it is always hard to honestly appraise our own products or value. I have been amazed at the movie industry trying to analyze why movie going has declined. They have an amazing number of excuses, none of which is that they have been making movies no one wants to go see. Likewise, the car industry with their analysis of why their market share is going overseas. They never seem to consider that perhaps they are making cars no one wants to buy.

In our case we must first admit that we really don't know very much about the product we are selling because we rarely sit through the funerals. Most of the time we are in the foyer or the parking lot waiting for the ordeal to be over. The best thing we could do would be to force ourselves to sit through the next six months of funerals just to see what we are selling. It is hard to self analyze but I really think the first thing we will discover is that people do not find much value to our product because, far too often, there is very little value there.

We produce cookie cutter affairs with the same tired formats and the same tired speeches by rather bored ministers just going through the motions of one more funeral. Most funeral directors know exactly when to show up because they have long ago memorized each clergy person's funeral speech and know when a certain poem appears, or text is read, it is near the end. We could plan the next sixteen funerals simply by knowing which clergy is delivering the eulogy.

Funerals happen because it is two o'clock on Tuesday. Very little planning or organizing goes into the service itself. We spend a great deal of time and energy on the minutia of details that surround the service, but the service just happens.

I recently officiated at a funeral for a long time friend. I had spent a great deal of time with the family in preparation for my remarks and wanted this to be a special time for the family. When I arrived at the funeral home I was met by a well dressed young man who gave me the typical minister's record—one of the most meaningless documents ever invented. He escorted me to the minister's waiting room and that's the last time I saw him. He had done the total work of a funeral director at a funeral service. The person who was to sing was looking through the hymn book with the organist searching for the hymns to be sung. When they found them they decided which verses to sing and they were ready. Just minutes before the service was to begin, a clergy person arrived to assist with the service. He breezed in, introduced himself and asked what he was suppose to do in the service. I asked if he had anything planned and he said he did not, but thought he would read the scriptures and the obituary. The material for that was in the clergy record. I said fine, then he asked what scriptures to read and wondered if he could borrow my Bible. As I sat on the platform watching the people gather and the family be ushered in, I thought, "My friend deserved more than this. He paid for more than this."

In our Celebrant trainings we tell our participants that even the worst commercial on television is scripted, planned, and rehearsed. Weddings are rehearsed. Children's plays are rehearsed. The only thing that we dare just start and hope it works out is the modern funeral.

One of the reasons this happens is that no one knows whose job it is. I have a picture of a possum that was run over by a car right in the middle of the road. The street crew that paints the lines came along and painted two yellow lines right over the body. That picture won the "Not My Job" award in Phoenix, Arizona. Not my job to move the possum, I just paint lines.

We really don't know whose job the funeral or family care really is. When I moved to West Texas several years ago, the funeral director asked me to tour his funeral home. He was very proud of the facility and liked showing it off. I think he had redecorated it about twenty-five years before that time, but to him it was still new. At the end of the tour, he put his hand on my shoulder and explained that he thought the funeral was between the family and the clergy, and he would honor that in every way. What he was really saying was, "I will embalm bodies and park cars, the rest is up to you." He was out of the loop, and whatever happened was up to me.

The result is the clergy own the funeral. We gave it to them lock, stock and barrel. Why? I have no idea. When? I think it happened so gradually no one can date it. But the clergy own the major thing you have to sell. This is a strange world indeed. The funeral director sells the product, the family pays for the product, but the clergy owns the product. Our role is to stand in the back of the room, or the parking lot, and hope it all goes well. Our standards are so low that if no disaster happens, it was a good funeral. The family might have been totally missed. The audience might have been bored to tears, or mad, but nothing fell over and the police escort was on time—good funeral.

The Challenge of the Clergy

That brings us to the next great challenge we must face. That is the challenge of the clergy. There is no easy way to say it, but the clergy are killing the funeral. There are exceptions, of course, and some do a wonderful job in caring for families and personalizing the funeral. But the vast majority either have one or two sermon templates and only change the name at the top, are locked into their denominational rituals, or see the funeral as an ideal time to evangelize. Every funeral director I have ever talked with knows this and we gripe about it constantly, but that is as far as we know to go or dare to go.

In defense of the clergy, we are not trained in this area. Most seminaries do not offer much, if anything, about death, dying or the funeral. The first funeral I attended as an adult, was one at which I was supposed to officiate. Fortunately there was an older pastor assisting and he told me what to do. I not only did that one the way he said, I did all of the next twenty years of funerals exactly that same way. No one ever suggested anything else. There is even a little black book full of templates to use at funerals, weddings, and any other type of function to help mold the clergy into performing cookie cutter affairs in all settings. It takes some real doing to break through that comfort zone and get the clergy to see the need to innovate.

I still shudder when I remember speaking at a funeral several years ago of a lovely young mother who had been murdered. We found out the next week that her husband was the one guilty of the murder, but I had suspected as much the day of the funeral. I stood there with all of the enthusiasm I could muster and told them what a victory this day was. She was in heaven and nothing else mattered. But almost everything else mattered. The family needed a safe place to mourn, not someone telling them they had no reason to cry. The family needed to establish the significance of their horrible loss, not someone trivializing it into nothing-ness. The family needed to establish the significance of this lovely person not someone indicating that her life here did not matter; all that mattered was the next one. I missed helping that family every way possible because that's all I knew to do.

The result is that people are tired of hearing the same tired phrases at every funeral. Those clichés or impersonal references become maddening when the family sits through an ordeal that misses their need, does not honor their loved one, and does nothing to acknowledge or give comfort to their pain. That, more than anything else, is causing people to avoid attend-ing or having funerals. They see no value in going through the same motions and hearing the same things over and over. When cremation came along, families responded, and I am convinced they did so because it gave them an out from having a traditional funeral.

New Zealand has a very high rate of cremation. Last time I checked it was 80%. They have never heard of immediate disposition of the body. When I explain that term to my friends there they are amazed and just cannot believe such a thing happens. Their families did not leave the viewing of the body or the funeral ceremony when cremation became the new way of final disposition. Why did that happen here and not there? A large percentage of their funerals are not done by clergy. The clergy there are locked into the rituals of the Church of England so they began to use lay people to present more personalized funerals. We will cover that phenomenon in more detail in a later chapter, but suffice it to say, that fact may well have made the difference in the impact of cremation on their funeral practices, as opposed to the impact it has had on ours.

On the surface it looks like we have painted ourselves into a corner. Our product is not turning on our customers and the major supplier of our product is locked into the status quo. Worse than that, the supplier controls the funeral and the funeral profession is afraid of making the clergy mad. So what, if anything, can be done? I think we can do a great deal. I think we can transform and restore the funeral, putting the funeral director back in their rightful place of honor.

Taking Back the Funeral

Let's face it, we are probably stuck with the cookie cutter eulogy. The clergy are probably not going to change very much. It is too easy to just change the name at the top of the template. That is how many of them are trained. A friend decided to become a minister after he retired as a funeral director. His seminary professor showed them a software template and bragged that they could plan a eulogy in less than ten minutes. That is probably not going to change, but that does not mean we cannot change the funeral.

The funeral director is the only person that can or will change the funeral. No one else is going to. We must and we can. However, the only way we can do so is by getting the funeral director out of the back of the room and involved in the funeral service itself. We need to take back at least a part of the product we sell and the family pays for.

I recognize that concept cuts across some very sacred traditions. Most funeral directors were trained that a good funeral was one where the funeral director was never seen or noticed. We are the ghost behind the scenes taking care of the details. I also recognize that most funeral directors are not just comfortable with that arrangement, they are horrified at the thought of having to be seen or...gasp...heard.

I hate to be the bearer of these tidings, but the family needs to see their funeral director. They bond with the first one that comes to serve them and expect that one to walk with them through the whole experience. We walk with them to the scariest part and leave them alone at the very time they need us the most.

A woman was sitting with a friend in the chapel where the friend's husband lay in state. The woman's daughter happened to be the funeral director and the daughter had a rather loud voice. The two women could hear the daughter talking in the office and the woman said she would go tell her daughter to speak softer. The widow said, "Oh, no don't do that. I need to hear her. I need to know she is back there." Funeral directors really don't know how important their very presence is to a family.

I talked a very reluctant funeral director into sitting with the family during the service. The first time he did so was a funeral for a police officer who had been killed in the line of duty. The service was in a gym and the crowd was large. Soon after the service began the four-year-old son of the officer needed to go to the bathroom. The funeral director took the boy by the hand to the restroom and back. He was amazed at how many people made it a point to tell him how great it was that he was there for that little boy. Had that been a funeral as usual that funeral director would have been in the parking lot shooting the breeze waiting for the cue he knew this particular minister would use at the end of the service. What a missed opportunity to serve that would have been. How many thousands of missed opportunities have we allowed since we decided our job stopped at the back door?

If the eulogies are not going to change then we must learn how to wrap personalization around the cookie cutter eulogies. We need to isolate the eulogy to be just a part of the whole service and not the service itself. That will take some doing but I think it can be done. It cannot be done radically or all at once, so I have devised a five year plan of action.

Turning the Titanic

The plan starts with the funeral director training and preparing the staff for an entirely new role. Many will balk at having to be seen, much less heard. At a recent funeral with one of our Celebrants, a young funeral director was asked to come forward during the service and hand out flowers to the family so they could place them in the casket. It scared the funeral director almost to a faint. She turned the job over to one of the part time helpers and stood at the side of the room. This was way out of her comfort zone, just to hand a rose to a family member. It won't be easy, but it is necessary if we are ever going to rid ourselves of the cookie cutter affairs we all know are killing us.

It could also start with the funeral director pairing up with his/her buddy preachers. Every funeral director has pastors that they are especially close to and who would be willing to try something new. Explain the process to them and the reasons behind your move and start with the funerals they do in your facility. Ignore the hard heads we all have to deal with who will not like any change, especially if it infringes on their turf.

Step One: Master of Ceremonies

Every funeral needs a Master of Ceremonies. How we have not seen this need is beyond me. The funeral is the only gathering that does not have one. Why should the audience have to guess who is speaking or singing and why they are the ones doing so? We are a scattered society. The people have gathered from near and far and no one introduces the speakers. Their names are printed but what does that do? The music is piped in from who knows where, sung by who knows who, and no one bothers to explain what the music meant to the deceased or the family. People relax and get involved when they feel comfortable. They feel comfortable when they feel informed.

I served as Master of Ceremonies at the funeral of my dear friend, Arnold Dodge. He was one of the great men in the funeral world and more than an employer to all who worked with him. When I met with the family they told me Arnold had a "fun" song that just had to be in the service. Arnold's nick name was Jake and he had great fun singing an old Jimmy Dean song titled *I Won't Go Hunting with You Jake, but I'll Go Chasing Women*. Imagine that just being played with no explanation in the normal funeral! I explained the song and it became part of the personalization that honored his life. Someone should serve in that capacity at every funeral.

The Funeral Director as Master of Ceremonies

The natural person to serve in this capacity is the funeral director. The funeral should belong to the family and should be directed by the funeral director. That word is more than just a name in our title. Families hire us to direct them, which includes being a consultant, a companion, and it should include being in charge of the service. This is not some innovation that will make the clergy angry. Why should the clergy be upset by someone introducing them? We should explain that the audience comes from a scattered society and many will not know who is speaking or what connection they might have with the family. If they do not know, they are not really listening as much as they are wondering. If the clergy person wants to be heard, then an introduction is in order.

Assuming this role injects the funeral director back into the funeral. We leave the back of the room and stop being invisible while becoming a presence to the family when they need us the most. The role is one small step toward isolating the eulogy into one segment of the overall experience. It does not diminish the eulogy, but it does allow for other elements to be added. Those elements are the secret to wrapping personalization around the eulogy. Perhaps a model of how we do this will serve to reduce the fear and grow confidence.

Imagine I am the funeral director:

I ask the audience to stand while I lead the family into the room and to remain standing for a moment. When the family is seated I read:

*We gather to remember the little things that made
a special place in our heart.
To remember those happy times when we laughed and
those times when our hearts broke as one.
For who could put a price on memories?*

*We gather to share the pain
To hurt when you hurt without
presuming that our pain is the same.
To cry when you cry and not try to hide or
avoid our tears.
For tears are memories in motion.*

*We gather to give the gift of grief
To stand beside you in silence and not be
uncomfortable with your pain.
To allow you the gift of grieving this loss and
not lose patience
For grief is nature's way of healing a
broken heart.*

Good afternoon. My name is Doug Manning of the Manning Funeral and Tribute Center. We are here to remember and celebrate the life of Tom Hoyle. It is our hope that every part of this service will honor a life lived among us.

I am sure you would like to join me in saying to his wife, Kay, sons Phil and Thomas Jr., daughter, Jill, brothers Wayne and Allen and his extended family of in-laws, nieces, and grandchildren that you are in our thoughts and prayers because of your loss. We want to be available to you in any way possible as you face the long journey of grief.

May I express the family's gratitude for your presence. The journey of grief is long and those who walk it should not have to walk it alone. In times like these nothing takes the place of friends. Your presence helps the family realize how valuable their loved one was to others and reveals the significance of his life.

We honor a man who, through his exuberant love of life, family and friends, touched many lives. We will stop to hear the stories, to laugh and cry together once again and to value the impact his leaving will have on each of you.

The music will be presented by _____

Or

The music to be presented was especially chosen by the family. (Tell why the songs were chosen)

Our minister today will be Rev. Stanley Jones. Rev. Jones has been the minister to this family for many years and I am sure his words will bring great comfort to us all.

After our time together here, you are invited to Rose Hill Cemetery for their final good-byes and military honors. A reception will follow the grave side ceremony here at the Tribute Center.

In the span of about three minutes I got the name of the deceased, the name of his wife and children, and the names of the extended family into the room. I made the place a safe place to grieve and acknowledged the grief of the family. I informed the audience about what was to take place and introduced the clergy person. Those three minutes can change the entire ambience of the service. Those three minutes can be the most healing thing that will happen to the family that day.

After doing this at the funeral home it is a simple step to suggest that it also be done for funerals done in the various churches. Most ministers will grow to love having the help and the introductions.

Step Two: Video Tributes

The funeral director can begin adding other elements. Increasingly more families request video tributes to honor their loved ones. The usual use for these is limited to visiting hours or played as a loop in the viewing areas. Sometimes they are played as the audience gathers and stopped when the family arrives. Not many people get to see the entire program and the family is not there when it is shown. This limits the impact and does not help the family. I love having the video as part of the service itself. This is best done by the Master of Ceremonies before the clergy begins the eulogy. Very few speakers like to interrupt their talks to inject something like a video. We do that by reading:

> As we begin, our firm has produced a video tribute that we wish to present at this time. May we pause as we spend a few moments remembering Tom's life.

> *Video Tribute*

> Rev. Jones will come now to give his words of comfort.

Step Three: Closing Ceremonies

As we get more comfortable both being in front of people and injecting our role into the closed world of the clergy, we can begin to offer closing ceremonies. The types and methods are endless. They vary from simple candle lighting to placing items in the casket, to the family closing the casket. These ceremonies can be presented to the family during the arrangement conference and some can even be a marketable item. If the family requests a ceremony, the approach to the clergy is to simply say the family wants this and you do not wish to "burden" him or her with any additional duties so the staff will take care of it.

Step Four: Committal Experiences

I chose the word experience on purpose. If we want people to buy caskets and bury bodies, we must make the committal service become an experience that heals. The normal committal is rarely worth the drive. We stand around a grave while the minister reads a scripture and mumbles words we cannot hear and that is it. There is rarely any sound system or music available. There is rarely any ceremony except for those done by the military or someone from an organization, such as the Masons.

I dream of the day when there will be sound and music at the graveside. Modern technology makes that as easy as an MP3 player and some speakers that run on batteries. Sound systems are now small and portable. The only excuse for not having these elements is our own inertia. Isn't that a fancy word for laziness?

I dream of the day the funeral director will step up when the minister is finished, thank him or her for their words and then lead the group in some kind of meaningful closing experience. Such as:

Hallowing the ground

When an old monk was asked why he cared for the ancient graves and why he cleaned the stones to preserve the writings carved there. His reply was simple, "they still have their names. They will always have their names."

From this day forward this place will bear the name of Tom Hoyle. It is here that his name will be honored by those who love him. It is here that he will be remembered by generations yet unborn. This place means he will always have his name.

When Chief Crazy Horse was asked where his home was, he replied, "My land is where my people are buried." He fought valiant wars to defend the burial grounds of his people.

For in those sacred grounds he found a connection with his heritage and felt like he belonged to a family.

There he found the hope that he too would be so honored and remembered. In this hope he found the courage to live.

From this time on this land will also be sacred to you.

For it is here that Tom's body returned to the earth from which we all came. It is here that he became one with the earth and with the universe.

It is here that generations to come will find a connection to their roots. They will come here and feel the sense of belonging to a greater force called family.

It is here that many will come to feel the presence and the love shared in life. Some will come often. Others may come only on rare occasions, all who come will be blessed.

It is here that we show honor to the memories of a life that touched us and remains alive in our hearts.

May we therefore hallow this ground by placing your individual flowers here and, by that act, pledge to remember and honor him for as long as you live.

(Song of choice plays)

This is now the earthly home of Tom Hoyle, and like Chief Crazy Horse our home is also where our people are buried, and we are standing on holy ground.

These steps may sound extreme and may scare us, but the only person who can, or will, change the funeral is the funeral director, and it cannot be done from the back of the room or the parking lot.

Challenge of Diversity

What isn't tried, won't work.
– Claude McDonald

Chapter Twelve

The Challenge of Diversity

I bought some socks recently. I don't know how I missed the fact but they do not make socks that fit individual feet anymore. They are size 9-12. No one makes a size 11 sock. That means none of us have socks that fit. We have socks we must stretch to fit. The same thing can be said about funerals. We operate in a "one size fits all" mode. We only offer religious funerals. Some more religious than others, of course, but most funerals are religious in nature and done by some kind of clergy. We have not given very much, if any, thought to funerals for those who are not particularly religious. Those multitudes of people who say they are spiritual but not religious, which means they have a faith but do not relate to organized religion or denominational trappings.

It seems we have given very little thought to making funerals fit the lifestyles of the people we serve. We do not seem to realize that people who are not connected to some religious group or organization are not comfortable being squeezed into our one-size-fits-all box. They are also not comfortable being around ministers. I always found that to be disconcerting. As soon as someone found out I was a minister their whole demeanor and language changed. They were uncomfortable, and so was I.

I remember suddenly realizing that I was sitting next to the beer tub at a wedding reception and no one would come near the tub as long as I was there. I finally left so they could enjoy themselves and the tub was under attack before I got to the door. People who are not around ministers do not know what to do or say when in their presence. When our one-size-fits-all program forces a family, who has never been a part of a church, to accept one of our "rent-a-ministers", they are on edge and spend the whole time trying to convince the minister that their loved one was a good person, even if he or she never went to church. The focus is on their discomfort instead of on their comfort.

This is fast becoming one of our greatest challenges. Religious faith is not winning the battle for the minds and hearts of people. We are losing. That is hard to see because every town has one or two mega churches that fill their auditoriums for multiple services each weekend, and it looks like we are in a time of great revival of interest in the faith. The truth is we are "Wal-Marting" the church. We are building big and the bigger ones are killing off the little ones. Someone said, "Instead of being fishers of men, we have become keepers of the aquarium and we spend most of our time swapping fish." Those multitudes we see in the mega churches on Sunday are not new converts. They are fish stolen from some smaller and weaker church.

While all of this is happening, the fastest growing segment of the United States population are people who do not go to church at all. The number of people who checked "no preference" on their census cards doubled from 1990 to 2000. In ten years the number went from fourteen million to twenty-eight million and it will probably double again in the next census. If the "nons" as they are called, were a denomination they would be third largest behind Catholics and the Baptists. If they were a state they would be the second largest in the U.S.

There is a definite connection between church attendance and immediate disposition. In states where church attendance is low, immediate dispositions are high and growing. When church attendance is high the number is lower but still growing. The pattern is: people quit going to church but return for funerals and weddings. Then they stop returning for funerals and weddings. Finally they stop having funerals and weddings. That is where we are right now. The Baby Boomers will bring their parents back to church for their funerals, but many will not do so when they die. Their children are the X-generation. A recent religious survey showed that 80% of the X-generation have never stepped inside of a church. Our one size fits all "rent-a-minister" concept will never work for the next two generations.

If fifty percent of our customers were Chinese would we refuse to present funerals that fit their cultures? No matter what the local ministers might think, we would offer Buddhist services. At least fifty percent of the people in every city or town do not go to church. We cannot afford to ignore that fact or those families, any longer. They are already the first ones to leave us. For many years it was not socially correct for a family to not have a funeral. As soon as that barrier broke down, those we have neglected led the parade toward minimal or no services and immediate dispositions.

Celebrants

I toured Australia on a speaking tour in the early nineties. At every stop I ran into people who called themselves Civil Celebrants. I found out they were lay people who performed funerals and weddings, primarily for families who were not affiliated with any faith group and for families who wanted a different type of service for a loved one. I became more and more intrigued as the tour went on. I continued to think about that concept after I returned home.

A few years later, I toured New Zealand. By that time, I was convinced that we needed Celebrants in the U.S. and Canada. I was not off the plane more than twenty minutes before I was pumping the funeral directors there about the Celebrant concept. I discovered that a few years prior to my tour a woman in that area had started writing articles and a book about the fact that there were no funerals for non-religious people like her. In response, both countries started licensing what they called Civil Celebrants. Since the church attendance in both countries is not strong the idea has dominated the funerals and weddings. Approximately sixty percent of the funerals in Auckland, New Zealand are done by Celebrants instead of clergy. I understand the numbers are similar in Australia. I learned as much as I could while I was there. I attended a Celebrant funeral in New Zealand. The more I saw the more I liked what I saw.

I came home convinced we needed Celebrants in North America. I tried to get some organizations interested but had no luck. Finally, Glenda Stansbury and I decided to see if we could do it ourselves. We asked the New England Institute at Mount Ida in Boston, Massachusetts to let us use their building, sent out a brochure and fifty people showed up. We were overwhelmed, of course, but we were on our way. There were even four nuns there. We thought they had not read the brochure very well but they told us they saw this as outreach. They realized if they learned how to minister to families during a death and the funeral, they would have a much better chance of reaching them later.

Since that first session we have continued to offer training in what we call Certified Funeral Celebrants. Glenda built the training and is the Dean of the training institute that offers the courses around the U.S. and Canada. I go along and offer a speech or so, but the real training and the care and feeding of this concept has been hers from the start. For that reason I asked her to write some thoughts about what Celebrants are and how they can help transform funeral service.

The Celebrant Concept
By Glenda Stansbury

The phone rings and on the line is a funeral director from one of the firms in my city. The words are: "Glenda, we have a family who needs you". And the excitement and the experience begins all over again. There is nothing in my wide and varied career that gives me more joy or satisfaction than serving as a Celebrant for a family. It is the seminal opportunity to do something that is meaningful, lasting and powerful in funeral service. I cannot wait to go see the family, to hold the family meeting and then gather the stories, the memories, the moments and the ceremonies into a service that will honor the dead and comfort the living.

After the first training in 1999, it became apparent that we had found an avenue and a process for preparing people to serve a wide variety of families. The historical practice in the funeral profession of finding an outside clergy person who was willing to do a funeral for a non-church member is deteriorating. Many ministers are no longer willing to do services for people outside their church.

However, the larger problem is that families are growing dissatisfied with the lack of personalization or the insistence by the minister on using their denominational rituals, scriptures or espousing their beliefs. These families are the ones who are choosing immediate disposition and then planning a memorial service that reflects their beliefs and honors their loved one at another time away from the funeral firm. We understand that that not only hurts the funeral profession by taking away potential business, but hurts the families because their needs are not being met by the professionals they trust in the funeral experience.

It has been well documented that the Baby Boomer generation has a different level of expectation for events and experiences in which they take part. Everything from weddings to internet blogging to social networking to cell phone ring tones demands a personal touch or flair. This generation was raised on questioning conventional ideas and breaking traditional rules. Now that they are reaching middle age and planning funerals for their parents or other family members, they bring a higher demand for unique, special and individualized service. They are no longer content with the mantra "we've always done it that way before."

We continue to improve, expand and modify the training, but our initial goal has never changed—our Funeral Celebrants are trained to provide a funeral service that reflects the life and beliefs of the deceased and the surviving family. Each Celebrant is charged with the responsibility to create with the family a unique, personalized and individualized funeral service that incorporates meaningful ceremonies, rituals, readings, music and reflections on the life of the deceased, regardless of their church affiliation, religious beliefs or lack thereof. We call ourselves Certified Funeral Celebrants but we recently added the title of Life Tribute Professionals. We've heard story after story from our Celebrants about amazing services, life-changing experiences, opportunities for healing among families and incredible moments of grace that took place during the process of putting together a service.

We established the In-Sight Institute as the training division of Doug's publishing company, In-Sight Books, and each year we travel North America offering as many as seven trainings a year.

We attract a wide variety of professionals with backgrounds such as funeral professionals, chaplains, clergy, social workers, educators, actors, writers, hospice personnel, and students. The common denominator among all Celebrant trainees is the desire to provide a well-done, thoughtful and meaningful funeral celebration for a family.

Many firms have Celebrants on staff—a funeral director, a pre-need professional, or a bereavement specialist—who also fulfills the role as a Celebrant. The most successful situations are the firms who have two Celebrants available so one can act as a Master of Ceremonies and one can serve as a Celebrant. There are hundreds of "independent contractors" who are ready and willing to work for any firm that calls and takes each assignment as a serious responsibility to meet the needs of the family and to honor the firm that has hired him/her.

Our trainings are a three day face-to-face experience with a group limited to thirty participants. Our goals in the trainings are:

1. To ground the participants in the value of the funeral and to understand what a funeral needs to do for families in grief.
2. To reveal the importance of the funeral director and his/her impact upon a family and show how Celebrants can work in concert with them.
3. To emphasize that personalization is more than a product or staging of an event and to focus on the importance of creating meaningful rituals and ceremonies.
4. To train the Celebrant in conducting a family story-telling time. These experiences have proven to be the most powerful and healing part of the Celebrant funeral experience.

After the training, Celebrants are given a certificate designating them as In-Sight Institute Certified Funeral Celebrants. We keep a data base of all practicing Celebrants and can help a funeral home or a family find one in their area. We offer ongoing support through training, resources and the on-line Celebrant Community where Celebrants can share experiences and assist each other with service development.

The majority of the time a Celebrant will be called to serve a family when it is expressed during the arrangement conference that the family has no church affiliation or does not want the traditional religious-based service. However, Celebrants can be utilized in so many different settings—a traditional service, a memorial service, a holiday gathering, a graveside service, a special Life Tribute service during a wake or rosary—the opportunities and options are unlimited.

The results of a Celebrant funeral can be long-lasting. Countless families have come back to a firm to discuss pre-need arrangements so they can specify that they want a Celebrant to do future services. Many of our Celebrants are requested to do a second or even a third service for the same family, sometimes years apart. The family remembered how wonderful and special the service was for their loved one and they wanted to have that type of service again. Firms are now advertising the fact that they have Celebrants available for families and putting the service on the GPL as a service choice.

One of our funeral director Celebrants in Canada told us that funerals have changed her entire community. Now over 300 people may show up for a service, when they used to have 50 who would make the effort to attend. Word has gotten around that the services that this firm offers are unique and meaningful and people make the time to be a part of the experience. Some of our large firms who have several Celebrants on staff or on contract now have a full time Celebrant Coordinator who works to match a Celebrant with each family who requests one.

Funeral homes can offer the latest in on-line memorial books, web casting, video services, dove releases and personalized service folders but, until the service is focused on the life lived, all of our efforts are merely set design. Our profession seems to have gotten a little lost in the variations of merchandise and technology, when what a family really wants and needs, and will gladly pay for, is the opportunity to have someone honor the life and legacy of their loved one. That is what brings families back to a firm.

The most important hurdle that each Celebrant encounters is the funeral director's willingness and ability to articulate the options and offer the choices. When a family begins the arrangement conference by stating that they do not have a church or a clergy person, rather than automatically reaching for the Rolodex to find a "rent-a-minister", the funeral director must instead explain what a Celebrant is and what a Celebrant can do. Most families are immediately relieved that there is a trained professional who can help them honor the life of their loved one.

Inevitably we are asked several questions by funeral directors who are considering utilizing Celebrants.

"How much do Celebrants charge?"

The fee charged by Celebrants varies across the country and is almost consistently higher than the usual clergy "honorarium". There are two reasons for this. First, Celebrants will spend 8 to 10 hours preparing for a service, having a family meeting, working with the funeral director, creating ceremonies or assisting with music. Second, a clergy person is paid a salary to pastor a church. Within that salary is the expectation that the clergy will be available to the parishioners to "marry and bury". So, their honorarium for a service is truly that—a thank you, not a professional fee.

But beyond the hours spent or the cost, what we have found is that the telling the life story of the loved one is a priceless service. The issue is truly not the fee; the truth is that people will pay for that which has value to them.

"All of my families want a religious service"

Most of our families define themselves as "spiritual but not religious". They may find great comfort in prayers and scripture; they just do not want a theological or denominational emphasis. Using a Celebrant does not mean that the family does not have the ability to incorporate religious elements into the service. The difference is that the family chooses the ceremonies, readings, scriptures or music that is meaningful to them—not something that is automatically or ritually included in every service.

An easy way to determine how often you could offer a Celebrant to your families is this: go through your records from last year and count the number of times you called a "rent-a-minister" because the family did not attend a church and had no one to officiate. Whether that number is 5, 50 or 500, that is the number of times a Celebrant could have served your families.

"Won't the clergy get angry?"

The families who are served by a Celebrant are usually not a part of anyone's congregation, parish or temple. Increasingly we are seeing clergy who have determined that they will only do services for their members, so that leaves this growing number of people on the outside looking in and needing a professional who can conduct the funeral.

The second part of this answer is a little more difficult—your families need healing and meaningful services and it is in your best interest as a caring professional and a business person to find ways to meet those needs, regardless of what others might think or say.

While the acceptance of Celebrant practices is increasing and more funeral directors are recognizing that a significant portion of the community they serve is not affiliated with a church or a clergy person, there is still reluctance to embrace the idea of the necessity of having a Celebrant available for families. Change is slow in this profession but many forward thinking funeral directors are recognizing that they must change as the demands of the market changes.

All it takes is a look at the growing cremation with no service rate to know that families have seen what funeral homes have to offer and their response is increasingly, "No thanks, I'll do it myself". Unless we develop options, new services and creative ceremonies that fit this generation, funeral service as we know it may go the way of the horse drawn hearse and the home embalming machine. The first and best step that you can take for your firm is to offer Funeral Celebrants.

The bottom line is that the firms who are doing everything they can to meet the needs of their community and the families they serve are the ones who have embraced Celebrants.

-G Stansbury

Family Meetings

The developing of the Celebrant idea has been one of the most satisfying things I have ever done in my life. Seeing people become equipped to help families in their grief and hearing the reports of their experiences after they go back home and put the ideas to work is a thrill. There is one other aspect of our approach that I think sets us apart and probably becomes the most healing aspect of everything we do. That is what we call family story telling time.

The night before my grandmother's funeral, my father suggested that we all go visit her. We went to the funeral home, sat with her body and began to tell stories about her life and her impact upon our lives. I do not remember much about the funeral the next day, but I will never forget that night, nor the stories we told. We did not realize it that night but we were beginning the process of keeping her alive. No one is dead until they are forgotten and we never forgot her. The stories kept her alive. Every time the family got together they told those same stories. I used to say that I not only knew the stories that would be told, I knew the order in which they would be told.

That night was so meaningful to me that I started offering nights like that to the families I served as a pastor. I would simply find a quiet place and gather the immediate family for a time of telling stories. Two families have flown me in to do the story telling time when schedule would not allow me to do the funeral. They had experienced one of the sessions in a past loss and had to have it again no matter how far I had to fly. A man thanked me last year for a family story telling time I led in 1975. He still remembered that night.

I really did not know the full power of these sessions until my father-in-law died. Both of his two daughters married ministers and neither of us wanted to take over so I did not try to arrange a story time. We had a very traditional funeral with crowds milling around the house prohibiting any chance for a conversation of any length. I hurt all the way home. There were so many things I wanted to say about him and so much I wanted to learn about him and I realized there would never be another opportunity for that group of people to be together in an appropriate place to tell the stories of his life. The stories were lost. Then I really understood the power of this time of remembering.

We made story telling a vital part of our Celebrant training. We spend a great deal of time showing our participants how to organize and conduct these sessions. We help them discover that a good family time gives the family all seven of the elements that we discussed in the first section of the book: Safety, Participation, Roots, Ceremonies, Reality, Significance, and Presence. We think these are vital to a family in grief. Our main emphasis is that even though a personalized funeral comes out of these sessions, that is not the primary reason nor force behind them. The main reason and value to the sessions is the healing of a family in grief and I don't know anything more powerful than these sessions. I cannot begin to relate how many reports we have received of families thanking our Celebrants for taking the time and organizing the family so these sessions could happen.

If we can offer a time of healing and a personalized funeral to families, it seems unthinkable that the funeral profession would have any hesitation whatsoever in accepting this new and timely idea.

Challenge of Our Fears

Who dares nothing, need hope for nothing.
– JCF von Schiller

Chapter Thirteen

The Challenge of Our Fears

The final challenge is the challenge of facing our own fears. I have been deeply involved in funeral service for almost forty years. I have spoken at conventions and conferences all over the U.S., Canada, Australia and New Zealand. After almost every conference or convention I see groups of funeral directors talking together about the new ideas they have just heard, how inspired or re-inspired they now feel, even how the materials presented are the answer we need to face the future. They are on fire and ready to go home and transform funeral service. Then they go home and leak. Nothing happens.

We could blame that on getting back into the busy world with no time to innovate. We could blame it on what innovation might cost, even though the innovations we offer in this book do not demand much, if any, cost. I am convinced the real problem is fear. We have never learned how to conquer our own fears. Roosevelt said "We have nothing to fear but fear itself" and that is certainly true in the world of funeral service. There is a passage in the Bible that says, "The fear of man sets a snare." We are trapped in our own fears. We seem to be like the man who swallowed an egg. He was afraid to move for fear it would break and afraid to sit still for fear it would hatch.

We Are Afraid of Promoting Ourselves or Our Work

One of the products we tried led us to a startling discovery. Most funeral directors are afraid to say anything good about funeral service or even their own funeral homes. We produced some radio spots for funeral homes to use in their advertising. We sent four spots per month so they would remain fresh. Most of the spots dealt with the grieving process but one spot each month talked about the value of the funeral or the funeral director. We found out most of our customers would not play the spots that promoted them or funeral service. They seemed to think the whole world is just waiting to accuse us of chasing ambulances.

We Fear Our Competition

Ours is a unique business situation to say the least. There were two million funerals in the US. last year and every one of them who wanted to use a funeral home were serviced. There is no unclaimed business opportunities lying unnoticed and untouched that we can go find and capture. The only way we can grow is by taking business away from a competitor. This leads to some very intense competition, of course. It also leads to a great fear of change. We seem to live in constant fear that any misstep could lead to our competitor taking away every family we serve. It also leads to constant criticism of our competitors. Most of the negative stuff about funeral service comes out of funeral directors talking about their competition. I cannot remember a time when a funeral director who met my plane when I arrived for a speaking engagement did not begin talking about how bad the "other funeral homes" were in his city. It usually starts before we are out of the parking lot. I could take what I have heard and write a much more condemning book than Jessica Mitford did. We need to conquer our fear. If we learn how to touch families at their point of need and do so with compassion, if we learn how to produce funerals that help folks face their grief journey, your competition doesn't have a chance of getting your families.

Fear of Incompetence

I really think this is the fear that does us the most harm. Most of us don't feel competent to deal with the task we have given our lives to perform. We do not know what to say to people in pain. We do not have confidence in what our very presence can do. Most of us went into funeral service with a real desire to help people, and somehow fear drove us to become masters of minutia, avoiding any emotional involvement.

There seems to be an idea that becoming emotionally involved with families will do us much harm. I don't think we should cry at every funeral, of course, but we certainly should cry at some of them. If not, we become so detached we cannot even feel at home with our own families. Of all the audiences I speak before, an audience of funeral directors is the hardest audience to move. We are so accustomed to holding our feelings in check that in those settings I have had to learn not to expect much response. I wish I could do a study on the long term impact this holding in of emotions has on the funeral director and his or her emotional well-being. Most of that comes from our fear of incompetence.

I can relate to that fear. I became pastor of my college town church when I was twenty-four and just out of college. I knew nothing and I am sure it showed. I went home every Sunday night knowing I had already told them everything I knew or could learn, and had no idea whether any of it was right or not. To make matters worse, people started coming to me for counseling. The only thing I knew how to do was to give them some scriptures to read and tell them to pray about it. The insecurity and incompetence could have ruined my life and my career. A couple of things made a difference.

First, I learned as much as I possibly could about what people were feeling when they were facing difficult decisions, relationships, and pain. There are libraries full of materials available so we can learn what to say and become comfortable responding to people. The more we respond the easier it gets. The more we understand that responding and feeling are not something dangerous to be avoided, we will find that it gives meaning and purpose to our lives and careers. Feelings aren't dangerous; sharing them does not lead to mental illness.

The second thing that helped me was learning that all I really had to do was be there and listen. As we've said before, healing always begins in the other person's bucket. People get insights into their problems as they talk. The real healing takes place inside of them and, most of the time, we have no idea what is happening when it is happening or how much good is being done. We must learn to trust that concept because there really is no way to feel competent when we are in the business of helping people. Since it happens inside of them there is no way for us to govern what happens, nor is there any way for us to measure the effect we are having. All of us live in a world of give and hope.

I have been walking with a woman whose daughter was murdered. We meet on Wednesdays when I am in town. Almost every time we finish a meeting I watch her walk away and realize I have no idea whether I helped her that day or not. I hope I did, but there is no way to measure what may or may not have happened inside of her as we talked. If we give presence and listen to stories we should go home at night and feel good in the knowledge that we have done our part, the rest is up to the family we touched.

We Fear the Clergy

Almost every new idea I have ever mentioned to funeral directors has been met with "What if the clergy does not like that?" I hear that every time I talk about the funeral director becoming the Master of Ceremonies at the funeral or just becoming a part of the funeral. The response is almost automatic. Someone will tell me that the clergy they work with would never stand for such an intrusion and almost everyone in the room nods in agreement. When I ask how they know the clergy would not like the idea, they have nothing to offer. Most have never tried a new idea out on their clergy, they just assume they won't like it and cannot take a chance on offending them by even asking.

We had to struggle against the same fear as we introduced Funeral Celebrants. It is assumed the clergy will be upset and see Celebrants as competition to them. I cannot remember a single time that we have presented the idea without that issue coming up.

There are several facts that rebut the issue quite well. Many of the funeral directors who have gone through our training have adapted the Master of Ceremonies idea even if they did not become active Celebrants themselves. To this date we have not heard one report of a minister being offended when introduced by a funeral director.

We have had very few reports of clergy being upset by a funeral home offering Celebrant funerals. Most ministers do not want to do funerals for non-church-going families. They are not comfortable doing so and realize the families are not comfortable with them. There are exceptions, of course, but they have proven to be rare. More and more funeral homes report that ministers are refusing to do funerals for anyone except their own church members and they are having a hard time finding ministers to do this kind of funeral.

I did a series of clergy conferences in both Michigan and New York. In both cases we held sessions in several locations around the state and attracted very good crowds. I think we had over 1,000 total participants in the New York sessions. I presented the Celebrant idea at every session and did not get a single negative comment from the clergy. It made sense to them. Several said they were pleased that someone was going to be there to minister to these families.

The clergy do not keep up with who is doing funerals. Funeral directors are the only people who read the obituaries and keep records. The only funerals most ministers notice are the ones they are called on to officiate. If it is not one of their flock they rarely would ever notice or care who was doing the service.

The real issue is what is behind our fear of the clergy in the first place. Somehow we got the idea that the clergy determine which funeral home their members use and if one got mad at us we would be out of business. I was a pastor for thirty years and recommended a funeral home one time in those thirty years. That was a very tragic murder of a man who had not been in our city very long and his wife really had no idea what to do. She asked and I gave her three names of the funeral homes in the area. If a minister tried to tell his or her congregation to use a certain funeral home, he or she would have more negative feedback than anyone would ever want. I have always been rather amused at how funeral directors fear and fawn over pastors, and ignore the people who actually do have conversations about funeral homes on a regular basis. If a funeral director wants to romance someone who really counts, he or she should pay attention to the nurses in hospitals and hospices. They visit with families about funeral homes almost daily.

In all honesty we may have to deal with an unhappy clergy person or so. We may have to stand up and let them know the funeral is not their private domain. You sold it, the family paid for it, and you must do what they want and you must have a way to serve all people in ways that meet their needs. We must find the courage to take our business back. Every funeral director that I have talked with agrees that the clergy are doing damage through lack of training, lack of information, or lack of ability to change. Do we dare let fear keep us from taking the actions we need to save our profession and serve families?

I remember an older funeral director who sat through a two day in-house training we did for a large funeral home finally asking "What if the clergy don't like these ideas?" My response was:

> *So what if they don't? The clergy do not sign your pay check. The families do that. We need to ask ourselves what business are we in. Are we in the business of keeping some clergy happy at all cost? Are we in the business of letting fear keep us from rocking any boats and keeping peace no matter what? Or are we in the business of serving people?*

The future belongs to those funeral homes that will say, "Whatever it takes. No matter what battles we have to fight. No matter who we might have to disagree with. No matter what we have to learn and how hard it is to get comfortable with new ideas, this funeral home will meet the needs of the people we serve."

I am convinced that when we learn to touch people where they hurt the world will once again come to our door to be touched.

Search and you will find that at the base and birth of every great business organization was an enthusiast, a man consumed with earnestness of purpose, with confidence in his powers, with faith in the worthwhileness of his endeavors. – B.C. Forbes

Guide for Facilitators

This training resource may be used with the book, the DVD or a combination of the two. The questions are structured to apply to the divisions in the DVD while grouping several of the chapters into a discussion questions.

We are providing some guidelines and suggested discussion questions to help plan a series of training sessions or classroom experiences. You may decide how they apply to your audience/students and how to adapt them to fit your needs.

There are several ways to approach the presentation:

- Show tracks from the DVD and use the book for the discussion questions.
- Assign a chapter from the book, use small segments of the DVD presentation for emphasis and use the book for discussion questions.
- Present concepts from each chapter of the book and lead a discussion.
- Show a segment from the DVD and lead a discussion.

Setting

Any training session is dependent upon the setting and comfort level established for the participants. Assuring that your setting is in a place with minimal distractions or interruptions, and a place where participants feel free to share, will go a long way to providing a successful session.

It is always important to allow time for participants/students to "get their voice in the room". Whether that means introductions, sharing experiences, or reflecting on the previous session —it is vital that each person has a chance to speak and be spoken to.

Three Basic Principles for Trainers of Adults

1. The environment must promote interaction, informality, and comfort:
    - Round tables
    - Refreshments

- Room to move around
- Reliable starting and ending times

2. The climate must be open, nonthreatening, and pleasant:
   - Address anxieties or concerns
   - Urge participation and involvement
   - Use accumulated experiences as a springboard for discussion

3. The task must be relevant:
   - Relate the topic to their experiences
   - Watch for "furrowed" brows
   - Devote time to questions and other points of view

Adult learners have some unique qualities that every facilitator needs to keep in mind:

- Adults see themselves as self-directing, responsible grown-ups.
- Adults have more experience and more to contribute.
- Adults are predisposed to learn from life's problems. They seek practical results from learning.
- Adults learn by doing and by the use of a variety of methods.
- Adults must want to learn. They chose to come to the training, and it may be wise to check out why they came and what they are seeking.
- Adult learning is an ongoing and continuous process.
- Adult learning can be threatening when it means change.
- Adults learn best in an informal environment.

Section One: The Value of the Funeral

DVD: Disk 1   59:00 minutes
Book: Chapters 1 – 8, Pages 11 – 39

1. Doug has identified seven elements that make the funeral valuable. Please list them and indicate how each of them applies to you and/or your funeral practice?
2. Of all the elements, which one do you believe needs the most emphasis in your profession?
3. Of all the elements, which one do you believe is the most difficult to assure that it is consistently part of the service provided to families?
4. What phrase will stay with you after reading/seeing this section? Why?

Section Two: The Challenges

Challenges of the Role of the Funeral Director

DVD: Disk 2 Track 1   40:22 minutes
Book: Chapter 10, Pages 48 – 70

1. List some of the "touches" that Doug described that historically were a part of the funeral profession.
2. What does the phrase "quiet dissatisfied" mean to you and the future of the profession?
3. Describe how the concept of buckets can apply to you and how you approach dealing with families.
4. Discuss some of the ways funeral professionals could improve their knowledge of their customer.
5. Discuss some of the ways that mortuary school programs could improve their students' comfort level with working with families.
6. Reflect on the first call procedures at your firm. Do you feel that your practices are effectively touching people or "filling the gaps"?
7. Reflect on the arrangement process and location at your firm. Do you feel that your practices convey a sense of safety and warmth to your families?

8. Reflect on the aftercare program at your firm. Do you feel that your practices are effectively sending a message of care or follow through?

Challenge of Our Product

DVD: Disk 2 Track 2 23:43 minutes
Book: Chapter 11, Pages 71 – 85

1. Discuss the effects that the clergy have had on the funeral profession and service to families.
2. Reflect on services when a clergy person provided a meaningful and personalized service for a family. Reflect on services when a clergy person failed to provide a meaningful and personalized service for a family. How did the families respond in both cases?
3. Discuss your reaction to the concept of funeral director as Master of Ceremonies.
4. Reflect on the model presented in Chapter 11 and discuss if that could be implemented in at least some services at your firm.
5. Discuss other new and significant ceremonies that you have incorporated into services for your families. How did the families respond?
6. Discuss new and significant ceremonies that you would LIKE to incorporate in services for your families. What is holding you back?

Challenge of Diversity

DVD: Disk 2 Track 3 17:45 minutes
Book: Chapter 12, Pages 87 – 99

1. What impact have you seen in your community relating to the growth of the "nons"?
2. Reflect on the number of times that you have utilized a minister for a non-churched family in the past year. Discuss if a Celebrant could have filled that role.
3. Have you heard the term "spiritual but not religious" from families you serve?

4. Discuss your understanding of Funeral Celebrants and how they serve families.
5. Discuss the drawbacks to utilizing Celebrants, if any.
6. Discuss the benefits to utilizing Celebrants, if any.
7. Reflect on how a family meeting concept could be incorporated into the process of serving a family.

Challenge of Our Fears
DVD: Disk 2 Track 4   13:03 minutes
Book: Chapter 13, Pages 100 – 109

1. There are several fears listed in this chapter. Discuss which ones seem to be the most complex or largest stumbling blocks to making needed changes in your profession.
2. Which of these fears could you address and find a solution for immediately?
3. Which of these fears could you address and find a solution for in the long term?
4. Which of these fears could be addressed by local/state/national associations?
5. Which of these fears could be addressed by further training in the mortuary school programs?

Notes

Notes

Notes

About the Author

Doug Manning

Doug's career has included minister, counselor, business executive, author and publisher. He and his wife, Barbara, are parents to four daughters and have been long-term caregivers to three parents.

After thirty years in the ministry, Doug began a new career in 1982 and devoted his time to writing, counseling and leading seminars in the areas of grief and elder care. His publishing company, In-Sight Books, Inc., specializes in books, video and audio productions specifically designed to help people face some of the toughest challenges of life.

Doug's latest efforts have been on the internet as he has become a blogger with his new website dealing with issues in the areas of grief and elder care. The Care Community is a website provided by In-Sight Books, Inc. free of charge to any who wish to join. It is designed to be a resource of help and support for people in grief or involved in caring for an elderly loved one. Read Doug's blogs and respond with your own experiences. Visit www.TheCareCommunity.com.

Doug has a warm, conversational style in which he shares insights from his various experiences. Sitting down to read a book from Doug is like having a long conversation with a good friend.

For a catalog or ordering information:
In-Sight Books, Inc.
800.658.9262 or 405.810.9501
OrdersAndInfo@InSightBooks.com
www.InSightBooks.com

Visit TheCareCommunity.com for Doug's blogs on Grief and Elder Care

Selected Resources from
In-Sight Books

By Doug Manning

Building Memories: Planning a Meaningful Funeral
*Building Memories: Planning a Meaningful Cremation
    Funeral*
The Continuing Care Series
Don't Take My Grief Away From Me
Lean On Me Gently: Helping the Grieving Child
The Power of Presence: Helping People Help People
    Book or DVD
Sacred Moments: A Minister Speaks About Funerals
The Special Care Series
Thoughts for the Lonely Nights journal and CD

Other Resources from In-Sight Books

I Know Someone Who Died coloring book
    by Connie Manning
The Empty Chair: The Journey of Grief After Suicide
    by Beryl Glover
Memories Too Few: A Letter to Parents About Pregnancy Loss
    by Kathy Manning Burns
The Shattered Dimension: The Journey of Grief After Suicide
    video by Beryl Glover
Comfort Cards bereavement card collection

For a complete catalog or ordering information contact:

In-Sight Books, Inc.
800.658.9262 or 405.810.9501
OrdersAndInfo@InSightBooks.com
www.InsightBooks.com

*Funeral Homes may also order In-Sight Books products from your
Dodge Company representative or by calling The Dodge Company
at 800.443.6343*